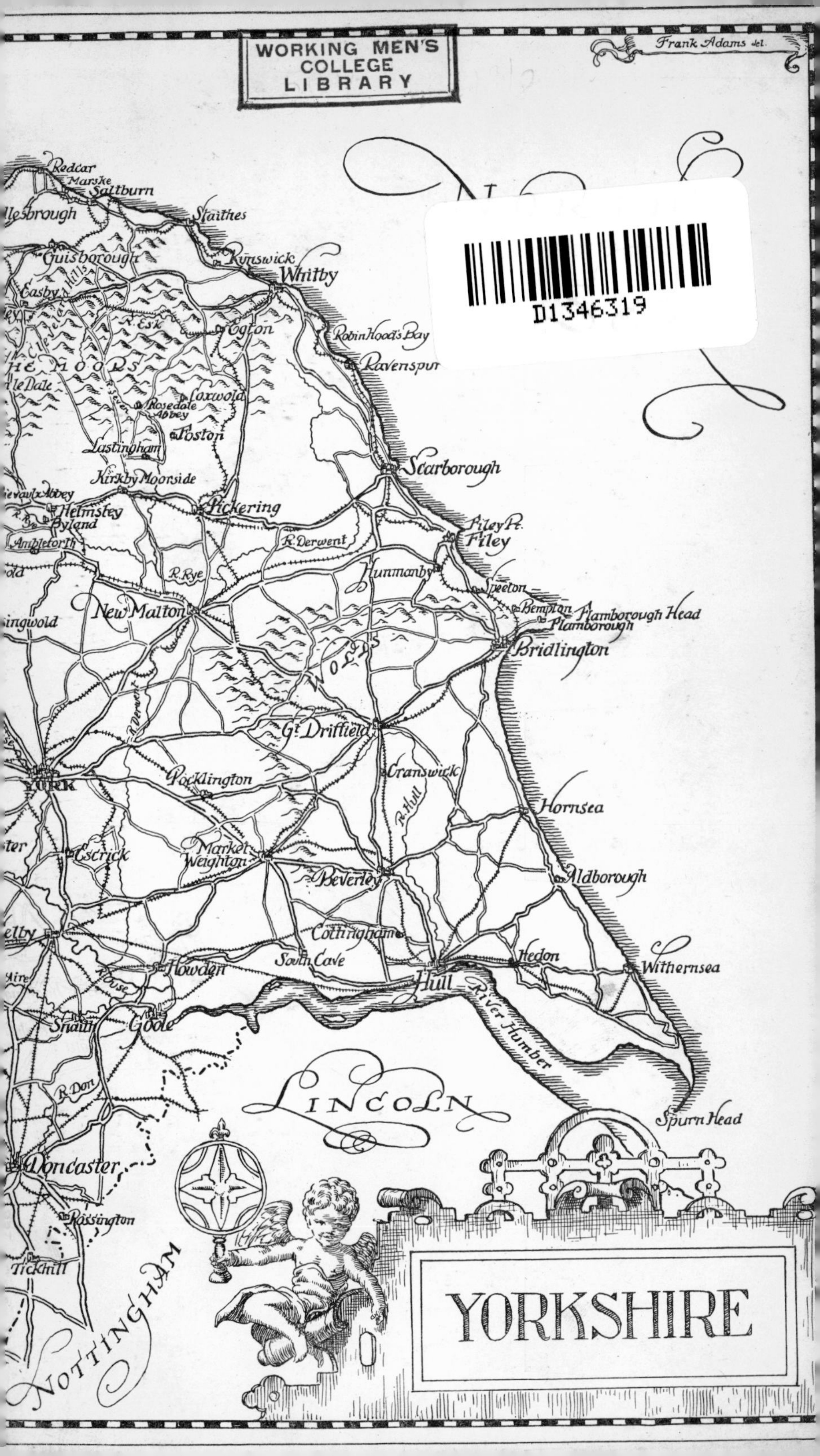
Frank Adams del.
Redcar
Marske
Saltburn
Staithes
Guisborough
Runswick
Whitby
Easby
R. Esk
Egton
Robin Hood's Bay
Ravenspur
Rosedale Abbey
Lastingham
Kirkby Moorside
Pickering
Helmsley
Byland
Ampleforth
Scarborough
R. Derwent
Filey Pt.
Filey
Hunmanby
R. Rye
New Malton
Speeton
Bempton
Flamborough Head
Flamborough
Bridlington
WOLDS
Gt. Driffield
Cranswick
YORK
Pocklington
R. Hull
Hornsea
Escrick
Market Weighton
Beverley
Aldborough
Cottingham
South Cave
Howden
Hull
Hedon
Withernsea
River Humber
Snaith
Goole
R. Don
LINCOLN
Spurn Head
Doncaster
Rossington
Tickhill
NOTTINGHAM
YORKSHIRE

THE WORKING MEN'S COLLEGE
AUSPICIUM
MELIORIS
ÆVI:
MDCCCLIV.
PRESENTED BY
PURCHASED.
R.E. TYLER DEL.
1913.
C.H. PERRY SC.

THE SPELL OF YORKSHIRE

YORK, THE MINSTER FROM THE OUTER WALL

THE SPELL OF YORKSHIRE

BY

J. CUMING WALTERS
AUTHOR OF 'THE CHARM OF LANCASHIRE,' 'ROMANTIC CHESHIRE,'
'IN TENNYSON LAND', ETC.

ILLUSTRATED FROM ORIGINAL DRAWINGS
BY
FRANK GREENWOOD

METHUEN & CO. LTD.
36 ESSEX STREET W.C.
LONDON

First Published in 1931

PRINTED IN GREAT BRITAIN

TO

HIS GRACE THE MOST REVEREND

WILLIAM TEMPLE

ARCHBISHOP OF YORK

WITH HIGH ESTEEM AND WARM PERSONAL REGARD

August 1931

PREFACE

THE title given to this volume defines not only its scope but its limitations. It deals with a county's 'spell' drawn from history, romance and lore. Yorkshire spreads so vast a canvas that a selective process was necessary, and its story is so long and complex that it could only be brought within the requisite compass by excluding what may be termed the more material elements. This will explain some omissions or the merely short and incidental references. In brief, these pages are intended rather for the lover of a literary pilgrimage than for the formal traveller. The 'spell' comes mainly from the past, and thus we are led to the consideration of famous events and old traditions associated with scenes of natural beauty and with places of bygone wonder.

I wish to express my indebtedness to Mr. Frank Greenwood for helpful suggestion and to Mrs. Jane Hilditch for useful research.

J.C.W.

August 1931

CONTENTS

LIST OF ILLUSTRATIONS

THE SPELL OF YORKSHIRE

CHAPTER I

THE COUNTY THROUGH THE AGES

THE Shire of the Broad Acres. The largest in England. Fancy toys with the pleasant idea (not quite correct) that by favour of Providence or chance of coincidence it contains as many acres as the Bible contains letters. Diversified, with long sweeping dales, dark rolling moors, craggy heights, wild torrents, sluggish rivers, heathery wildernesses, teeming cities, tiny hamlets, noisy centres of industry, remote and lonely farms. Studded with truculent historic castles, showing their broken turrets and crumbling walls. Strewn with desolate battle-fields. Glorying in rich minsters and mourning ruined abbeys. With an ancient capital where Caesars reigned and died. A treasure-house of relics, with the splendour and the pathos of an historic past. Yorkshire!

It displays essential character in populace, scenery, and language—that sonorous 'tawny' dialect, as it has been termed, in which much expressive Old English is conserved. It has its individual manners and its traditional customs. It has witnessed the making and changing of the nation's history, has had a part in fusions and severances, and has produced heroes in peace and war. Soldiers, statesmen, explorers, painters, poets, reformers, are among its great ones. Lustrous names shine out in its chronicles.

There is no date to the beginning of the story. The geologist probes, the archaeologist excavates, and the historian pieces together the fragments and makes a record. Pit dwellings at Danby Moor, Killing pits at Goathland, the Rudstone menhir near Bridlington, megalithic remains and devil's arrows at Boroughbridge, circular earthworks at Thornborough, and caves with mysterious markings, are among the reminders of vanished races and prehistoric times. And if, as Emerson said, England itself was a prize for the best race, this county of many invasions and seizures may be taken as supplying proof of that fact. Phoenician, Celt, and Goth had their turn, and the Roman came 'and looked into the eyes of a people that was to supplant his own'. For three centuries the Legions were there, camps and towers were erected, massive walls made; then the Roman went, leaving Saxon and Dane to wage their ferocious contests. The Saxon tilled, built, raised his altars; the Norseman destroyed and burnt. 'Woe to the realms which he coasted, where his black standard was seen'; 'before him was battle, behind him was wrack.'

The Norman arrived, victorious and harrying, determined to stay and rule. For centuries the Saxon was a serf; yet a day came when he dictated terms to the descendants of the Conqueror. Those are phases of England's chequered history, but no small section of them was inscribed in Yorkshire. And Tudor and Stuart chronicles continue a story which often throbs with excitement.

Statistics, otherwise dull and prosaic, derive a special interest from their exceptional character in this county of over 6,000 square miles, with 7 cities, 22 municipal boroughs, 150 urban district councils, 1,572 civil parishes. The three Ridings (*thridings*) have their own lord-lieutenants, magistrates, and constabulary; and there are six-and-twenty wapentakes, or hundreds. Place-names possess an atmosphere of legendary suggestion; history and romance are imbedded in them; old forms are reminiscent of the pagans who employed them. We detect a secret music in Kettlesing, Birstwith, Woodmanray, Keldholme, Bilsdale, and the like; we break into an enchanted circle at Pannal and the Crimple Valley; we touch on Nature's wildness at Ravensgill with its gorge and boulders, or at Aysgarth Falls where the Ure makes a foaming cascade as it tosses over the rocks, leaps from boulder to boulder, and sends its spray sparkling into the sunlight. And there is the stern serenity of the solitary hills over which a silvery mist softly creeps as the day passes.

Surprising are the contrasts to be witnessed wherever we turn—cities teeming with life and work, huddled little towns with blackening chimney-stacks lying under a blanket of smoke, coy villages half hidden, springing out suddenly round a corner, shyly peeping from a rocky verge; some with houses that go all a-slant down a narrow street as if they would topple over but for leaning shoulder to shoulder; or, such as typical Scarforth, standing gaunt and high, and like a watchful old friend summoning the scattered flock on the moors to a jubilant anniversary service. In one spot, like Aldborough, a tessellated pavement of old Rome may exude; in another, like Ribston, the charm may be in orchards with their 'pippins'; in another, like Thornton, one of the several so-called 'prettiest villages', artist or poet can find an idyll in the grey bridge over the curving river, the cluster of old-world cottages, the profusion of colour, everything permeated with the redolence of garden and mead. So to roam at will is to feast on beauty, revel in variety, to be stirred to wonder, and sometimes to catch the fleet illusion of a dream.

From the baldest and highest point of Mickle Fell, an old traveller remarked, you may survey 'a county half as large as Holland, and see beneath, small as toy-houses, the five great monastic ruins, and the six great castles which awaken memories of the Cliffords, Mowbrays, Lacys, and Scropes. The eastern cliff-ramparts, the bracing moors and fells, the green and laughing dales, the great manufacturing cities smoking like witches' cauldrons, lie before you, and those fair rivers, the Humber, Wharfe, Nid(d), and Derwent, stretch beneath the airy road their silver clues to the labyrinth to be traversed.' A later traveller, as valiant in climbing as in his power of description, etched a picture of the rugged grandeur of the uplands—taking Wharncliffe crags for inspiration, C. E. Montague traced an imaginary scrambler resting midway up a smooth and square-cut chimney, 'built for his use like a dream of desire', and viewing the moorland slopes below him 'sinewy and knotty with the twisted and notched roots that are still left of the chase where Gurth and Wamba talked together'. In silent intervals the wanderer would catch the sound of the broken notes of the Don: in the smoke-filled hollows he would see the distant chimneys of a sombre town. And in such a place, added Montague, you get an index or an epitome of north-west England, where the soil is more ancient and the ways of men's labour are more modern than elsewhere. 'For here alone, the edges of

WAKEFIELD CHAUNTRY

towns where work is all a manipulation of steam and electric power are frayed against ridges of rock that were old before the site of London was made.' A wanderer will make further discoveries to set him thinking furiously—a Street of Tombs, such as that between York and Tadcaster, commemorating the road-side cemeteries of the Romans; or medieval bridges and 'chauntries', such as those at Rotherham, at Otley, and at Kildwick, most venerable of all at Selby, and most quaint at Wakefield where the Calder is spanned, and where the sanctuary of Edmund Langley, a son of the third Edward, served 'to do dyvine service in the tymes of the plage for the secke people hither to resorte, that the rest of the parochians may com to ther paroch churche withoute danger of infection of the secke'.

The literary student may be led to speculate whether Shakespeare, familiar with names and places, was personally acquainted with scenes to which he alludes —the archbishop's palace at York, Pomfret Castle and its dungeon, Sandal Castle near Wakefield. He seemed to have some little particularity of knowledge concerning 'Gualtree' Forest:

> What is this forest call'd?
> The Gualtree forest, an 't shall please your grace.
> West of this forest, scarcely off a mile,
> In goodly form comes on the enemy;

and it was here that Falstaff took Sir John Coleville prisoner, whence he was sent on to York for execution. But as history supplied the dramatist with localities and circumstances, we need not seek far for explanation. 'Welcome, my lord, to this brave town of York', was Queen Margaret's greeting to her son, and the scene that follows is 'A Field of Battle between Towton and Saxton', the fierce and piteous incidents broken by that most pathetic of monologues of the hapless monarch, seated upon a hill, and meditating on the peace and sweetness of a shepherd's life. Middleham Castle figures next in the drama of *Henry VI*; and in the 'chiefest thicket of the park', long since disappeared, Gloucester, Hastings, and Stanley held conference to effect the escape of the King when he came 'hunting this way to disport himself'. A very precise piece of local history is woven into the conversation between Edward IV, the nobles, and the Mayor, the threads of which run:

K. Edward: . . . Thus arrived
From Ravenspurg haven before the gates of York . . .

Gloucester: The gates made fast!—Brother, I like not this . . .

Hastings: My liege, I'll knock once more to summon them.
[*Enter, on the Walls, the* MAYOR OF YORK *and his brethren*].

Mayor: My lords, we were forewarned of your coming,
And shut the gates for safety of ourselves:

. . . . .

Hastings: Why, master mayor, why stand you in a doubt?
Open the gates, we are King Henry's friends.

Mayor: Ay, say you so? the gates shall then be open'd.

K. Edward: So, master mayor; these gates must not be shut
But in the night, or in the time of war.
What, fear not, man, but yield me up the keys.

The reference has significance from the fact that whenever a king visited the city the form was observed of handing him the keys, and on departing His Majesty as formally returned them to 'master mayor'.

As for the people themselves, we are reminded that Marmion told King Jamie, 'Yorkshiremen are stern and bold', but that was in the hour of battle. A robust humoursomeness would more befittingly be given as the characteristic; it even became in time a stage-convention, the hearty, big-boned, good-natured, independent men, who loved gargantuan feasts with a toast:

> God bless us all an' mak' us able
> To ate all t' stuff what's on this table"

—men who delighted in open hospitality with a 'Here's to thee! Fond love, old son'; who stood staunchly by friends, fought foes hard, took a bluff with a laugh, and repaid it doubly. The type became absurd by exaggeration, but it had its origin in a general truth, and Dickens gave it illustration in his John Browdie. Better still is the example in history of the Leeds merchant, old John Harrison, who forced his way past the sullen Puritan musketeers, and, kneeling before their prisoner, King Charles, offered His Majesty with a smile 'a tankard of right home-brewed excellent ale'. There was the true Yorkshire touch about that, and the guards turned aside while the king lifted the lid of the flagon, and, lo! it brimmed not with nut-brown ale but with golden pieces. Leeds had been intensely loyal; Sir William Savile had offered a stout though unavailing resistance to Fairfax; royalist ardour was unabated in defeat, and it is said that a kitchen lass offered to change clothes with the king, and to lead him at nightfall to a house whence he could escape to France. To some such act is attributed the rise of the family who built Crosby House in Upperhead Row.

If loyalty, goodwill, and honest service are in evidence, so too is the shrewdness of Yorkshiremen. Cobbett, who could be bitterly critical and churlish, had nothing but praise for the type. The term of 'Yorkshire bite' he ascribed to their acuteness, their readiness in retort, their sharpness in business. 'Every one knows,' said he, 'the story of the gentleman who, upon finding that a boot-cleaner in the south was a Yorkshireman, and expressing his surprise that he was not become master of the inn, received for answer, "Ah, sir, but master is York too"!' He agreed with the adage, 'York, but honest,' and said that in the army he had found Yorkshiremen distinguished for their frank manner and generous disposition. 'In truth I long ago made up my mind that the hardness and sharpness ascribed to Yorkshiremen arose from the envy excited by that quickness, that activity, that buoyancy of spirits, which bears them up through adverse circumstances, and their consequent success in all situations of life.' At Beverley he admired their horses, shown off for speed and elegance on market days. The farmers and gentlemen assembled in the wide street, the grooms came, and the blood horses, coach-horses, hunters, and cart-horses were 'a sight worth going to see'; and there was praise for the adroitness, agility, and boldness of the grooms, 'each running alongside of his horse, with the latter trotting at the rate of ten or twelve miles an hour, and then swinging him round, and showing him off to the best advantage'.

Here a sure hand touches upon another marked feature, for the fame of Yorkshire for its horse-breeding is world-wide. There was a bitter jest of the rival county of Lancashire that when hanging was abolished for horse-stealing the population of Yorkshire appreciably increased, but that must be taken merely as recognition of the fact that the horse has a prominent place in the thought and affection of the county where the St. Leger has been run for over two centuries. Camden in his *Britannia* records that horse-racing took place in the forest of Galtres, east of York, from 1590, and the old saying of 'Bear away the bell' was derived from the custom of awarding a prize of a bell of gold or silver, attached to the gear of the horse, to the winner. In 1607, the inhabitants not to be deterred from their pleasure by such a mere obstacle as frosty weather, ran a race over the ice of the Ouse.

Sheep and wool come first in the economic scheme. When the old Radical saw thirty- or forty-acre fields with five or six hundred ewes, each with her lambs, and when he had a glimpse of Holderness, 'No wonder,' he exclaimed, 'that the Danes found their way hither so often!' 'For,' said he, 'there were fat sheep then, as there are now, and these noble churches and magnificent minsters were reared because the wealth of the county remained in the county, and was not carried away to the south to keep swarms of devouring tax-eaters and to cram the maws of wasteful idlers.'

He used to wonder, he confessed, why Yorkshire, which he had been told was sterile, raised beautiful cattle with short horns and straight, deep bodies. 'You have only to see the fertile county,' he explained. 'I have never seen any land to be compared with that on the banks of the Humber.'

To no inconsiderable section of the outer world it may be said that Yorkshire, apart from its big industrial centres, is only vaguely known. There is an elusiveness about some of the most recurring names, and Rievaulx and Jervaulx, glorious in their solitude, would not be familiarly spoken of as Rivers and Jervis; while Whipma-Whopma Gate at York might seem to be a jest in some medieval comedy. The sound of the horn at Ripon and Bainbridge would come as a startling surprise, as might the toll of curfew at York; while the sight of the Admiral of the Humber doubtless would be viewed with wonder. And is it still the custom, some one may inquire, for the parliamentary member for Hull to receive his allowance of ale, as Andrew Marvell did, and is it of the potency that he described or of the fine flavour that Taylor, the Water Poet, celebrated in verse? Of the many hills, the cataracts, the 'pots', the caves, how far extends the knowledge of the average pilgrim?—and who has that intimacy of the Striding Dales of which Halliwell Sutcliffe has written with such unfailing felicity and depth of knowledge—those highlands of eerie beauty and wonder 'raking up to wide-flung mountain-fastnesses lying remote from usual haunts, their people rooted in free, unspoiled acres'.

While history runs somewhat thinly in some of the largest and busiest towns, lore and legend richly course through many a remote and diminutive hamlet; names of saints, names of olden heroes, names of scholars, cling to secluded spots seldom reached except by the enthusiast. The valley of Coverdale is so small that some say only a Yorkshireman can find it for you; but there went forth from the small retreat a giant who strode the world as a Reformer in dark and dangerous days, Miles Coverdale, who translated the Bible, did the duties of a bishop, and braved the prison. The commercial capitals which have risen in strength and wealth dispense with romance; the true gold glistens among the dust of ruins, is secreted amid crumbling towers and broken arches and shattered altars.

There is much to discover, much to learn, much to do. Let us begin our adventure. The Great North Road stretches before us.

CHAPTER II

WITH THE WAYFARERS

A LONG road, beginning far from our starting-place and ending far beyond our destination: the Great North Road that has been ridden and tramped for two thousand years, that has echoed to the gallop of steeds and to the clang of armies on the march, and that has felt the soft tread of sandalled feet as pilgrims slowly made their way to the sacred shrines. And from age to age there have been leaves scattered on this highway, and as we gather them we can learn from the inscribed lines of some of the adventures which befell the travellers on their journeys.

It is the year 1654. Who comes riding from London 'into northern parts' on an August day, making careful note of town and country? A citizen of grave aspect who has lived through troublous times, and has watched the tragedy of one king and the restoration of another. He keeps a careful record of events in a secret diary, and his name is John Evelyn. He can tell us something of the Great North Road three centuries ago. Doncaster was 'a large fair town, famous for great wax-lights and good stockings', and Pontefract has a castle famous for sieges and the murder of a king—'It stands on a mount, and makes a goodly show at a distance.' The traveller alighted to drink at a crystal spring 'which they call Robin Hood's Well, and near it is a stone chair, and an iron ladle to drink out of, chained to the seat'. By way of Tadcaster there comes into prospect the archbishop's palace, ' a noble seat ', and then comes York. It is the second city of England, says Evelyn, ' watered by the brave river Ouse, bearing vessels of considerable burden on it ; over it is a stone bridge emulating that of London, and built on ; the middle arch is larger than any I have seen in England, with a wharf of hewn stone, which makes the river appear very neat '.

But it was the cathedral which held him fascinated, ' remarkable and worth seeing and of all the great churches in England best preserved from the fury of the sacrilegious '. He found it ' a most entire magnificent piece of Gothic architecture ', and he admired the screen before the choir, ' of stone carved with flowers, running work, and statues of the old kings '. ' They showed me,' he said, ' a Bible and Common Prayer Book covered with crimson velvet, and richly embossed with silver gilt ; also a service for the altar of gilt wrought plate, flagons, basin, ewer, chalices, patins, with a gorgeous covering for the altar and pulpit, carefully preserved in the vestry, in the hollow wall whereof runs a plentiful spring of excellent water '—no doubt referring to St. Peter's Well. Then he mounted the tower ' whence we had a prospect towards Durham and could see Ripon, part of Lancashire, the famous and fatal Marston Moor, the spa of Knaresborough, and all the environs of that admirable country '. But he thought the streets narrow and ill-paved, though the shops were ' like London '.

With its quaint phraseology, this gives us a picture of seventeenth-century York. Evelyn had, of course, more to see of the county itself. There was Hull ' situate like Calais, modernly and strongly fortified with three block-houses of brick and earth ', but to the fervent loyalist it was a reprehensible place—' infamous for Hotham's refusing entrance to His

Majesty'. Beverley, with its two stately churches, attracted his eye; yet it seems that his interest was even more excited in 'a very old woman who showed us the monuments, and, being about an hundred years of age, spake the language of Queen Mary's days', an episode worth recording. Then Evelyn gives his horse a pat, and it trots him over the border into Lincolnshire, where we bow farewell.

What this journey meant to a Londoner may be judged from the fact that it was a three days' ride to York, and two further days were needed for sight-seeing. The horseman doubtless prided himself on his expedition. The speeding-up in travel was not long to be deferred, and the Great North Road was soon to know the gallop of horses and the rumble of the coach. Not that we need give serious heed to one favourite story a century later, seized upon by Harrison Ainsworth in his romance of *Rookwood*, the breathless ride to York of Turpin on Black Bess; but Ainsworth knew the route, and the idea of such an exploit was probably derived from the actual feat of a certain John Nevinson who established a baffling alibi by appearing on York race-courses in what was deemed an impossibly short time after he had been picking pockets in London. Apart from the legendary ride, the conclusion of Turpin's story belongs to Yorkshire. Escaping from the Lincolnshire constables, he took refuge in Welton as John Palmer; and having in braggart fashion threatened to do a little shooting when suspected of horse-stealing, he was committed by the Beverley magistrates to York Castle for trial. There he was indiscreet enough to write a letter to his brother in Essex; identification followed; and on April 10th 1739, the highwayman was drawn on a hurdle to the place of execution, and after bowing mockingly to the spectators duly turned off.

Meanwhile the age of the stage-coach had arrived. We can understand De Quincey's rhapsody that it 'first revealed the glory of motion, through velocity at that time unprecedented'. Every moment, he said, there were shouted aloud the great ancestral names of cities known to history through a thousand years, York among the number, 'expressing the grandeur of the empire by the antiquity of its towns, and the grandeur of the mail establishment. All night long, and all next day, many of these mails, like a fire racing along a train of gunpowder, will be kindling at every instant new successions of burning joy'. And in this high vein he traced the journey northward for three hundred miles, 'like a fiery arrow let loose'.

Who next comes riding here, happy as a schoolgirl, keen of glance, apt of pen, eagerly anticipating meeting an honoured friend at the journey's end, and chattering all the way? She travels by one of these arrowy coaches, but is fain to linger, for she would look at castle, grounds, woods—nothing is to be missed, and there is a story everywhere. Is she not on her way to the supreme storyteller himself, the Great Unknown whose secret she already half-guesses and will penetrate if she can? A shrewd little lady, this, Mrs. Hughes of Uffington, travelling along the Great North Road two centuries after John Evelyn, and by no means finding it the dullest road in England as Sir Walter had declared it to be. She enjoys the ease of the new 'MacAdam' surface, and if, said she with lively humour, England were a Catholic country, 'MacAdam would have a votive chapel, which might be hung round with the legs of post-horses, the springs and wheels of carriages, the backs and hip-bones of travellers, and the hinder-ends of postboys', a delicious compliment. Pontefract Castle disappointed her: nothing left but 'two shapeless lumps like hussocks, and a few pieces of wall'. She admired the square towers of the fine old mansion of the Howards, but detested 'a pert, vile new house with green door and white stone front' which adjoined a noble fragment of gateway.

Then on to York, where she gave herself up whole-heartedly to admiration, except for the defacing of Micklegate Bar 'outraged by placards of "Buy Sisson's blacking" and "Sales of Beasts and Cattle"'. She resented, too, the well-intentioned effort of Mrs. Fry to convert Clifford's Tower into a prison for female convicts, and wished that benevolent lady had confined her intentions to Newgate 'instead of meddling with this noble remnant of the olden time'. But York Minster! 'The extraordinary magnificence of this glorious structure grows upon one, the more one gazes at it; it seems as if Giants had built it, and employed the fairies to finish it, so exquisite and minute are the carvings of the ornaments. The choir is far broader than in any Cathedral I have seen, and choir stalls so ample that Daniel Lambert might have sat in them at his ease.' And she saw the Quaker lunatic asylum with the pleasant gardens, the women at work; and she praised an old man for his early lettuce: 'he works in a hat trimmed with peacock feathers'.

So to Boroughbridge and Marston Moor, with memories of Cromwell and his reserves stationed in a wood; and next to 'Rippon' in the vale 'watered by the Yore'; thence to Studley, and to 'Fountain', where 'nothing can exceed the elegant neatness of the walks, and we were much pleased with the style of the whole, though old-fashioned and formal'. She was amused by a guide who pointed out 'Venus de Medicine' and 'Hercules strangling Anthony', and we can share her merriment. The vale into Masham she found 'very lovely', and she enjoyed twelve miles of beautiful country through Wensleydale to Leybourne, and thought Prior Aymer's lot must have been cast in a fruitful ground at Jervaulx. At Richmond her feelings were mixed. The country disappointed her, 'but the town is handsome, and the situation romantic and beautiful: there is a fine open square of good houses: there are few things finer than the massy ruins of the castle, the broad walk which surrounds it, and the Swale running wildly at the foot of the abrupt precipice on which the old towers stand'. Her native patriotism led her to compare it to Llangollen.

One special desire of the hero-worshipping lady had been to see Rokeby to advantage, and Scott had asked her to make a slight detour in order to witness the scene of his poetic romance. But capricious weather rather marred the enterprise—'the bright rainbows which had embellished our view for the last six miles brought rain'; luckily there was a timely clearance, and she walked by the side of the Greta 'under the precipitous rocks on which the mansion of Rokeby stands, and viewed the river dashing over large rocky fragments, and forming cascades till it reaches under a high single-arched bridge to meet the Tees'.

Four years later, when she paid a second visit to Abbotsford, she returned by Leeds, Wakefield, 'Newscam', Barnsley, Ravensfield, Conisborough, 'Rotheram', and Sheffield, duly recording her impressions. Leeds was 'an immence, dirty, smoaky town'; Barnsley 'thriving with great linen manufactories'; Ravensfield 'one of the most delightful places imaginable'; 'Rotheram' 'pleasant', Sheffield only 'one degree better than the abominable town of Birmingham'. The most detailed reference was to Conisborough Castle, perfect except for the roof, a massy tower of great strength, standing on an eminence above the Don, 'which winds through a lovely narrow valley, the banks clothed with woods and broken by rough ground covered with ferns and low shrubs'. She was attracted by the steep and giddy flight of stone steps and by the dungeon, 'which is so deep that the bottom is not visible', and it was impossible for her 'not to think of Ivanhoe and Athelstan, and to trace in imagination the road by which the supposed dead man came dashing along to join his own funeral feast'.

Though now and then we get the thrill of real adventure in reading such a journal a false glitter of romance tinges the good old days when coaches at mad speed rattled from London to York in forty-eight hours. Those who look back perceive the gay side, those who had experience realized a sombre truth. One traveller will tell us so. Down the road, with swing and swagger, comes six-foot-two, and he calls for his ale at the tavern, talks loudly to the bystanders, argues with the parson passing by, throws strange words to the village wiseacres, gibes at the Pope, and stands at the door to watch a heavily-coated coachman descend from his seat and strut about with arrogance. Little does George Borrow, the gipsy scholar and philosopher, the word-maker Lavengro, the lover of fisticuffs, and the sworn friend of Mr. Petulengro—little does he care for the puffed-up driver receiving homage from the stable-men. Aha! says he, to the little wiry fellow at his side, these bullies will soon have had their day, and he vastly enjoys seeing one of them thrashed; and then he ruminates that the coach itself will be in the lumber-shed ere long, that disenchantment will come, and that all England will be 'surrounded with roads of metal on which armies may travel with mighty velocity'. Then the philosopher, turned prophet, drinks up his ale, tosses his sixpence to the host, twirls his big stick, and with a jaunty air strides away.

And now, who is this blithe, bright-eyed young man, with an infectious laugh, abounding in energy, who comes along the Great North Road on a winter day, and while the horses are changed watches the guard and coachman stamp up and down and print off their shoes in the snow? He will never forget that journey, for with all his mirth he is a crusader, and he has come to Yorkshire with a stern purpose. He is a bridegroom of only a few months, and to the young wife left behind he writes letters in high spirits, telling her how 'we came round the clock, upon the Great North Road, to the performance of Auld Lang Syne, and it snowed, and snowed, and still it snowed, and never left off snowing'. He is full of hope and ambition, for this is Boz, and he has heard of schools up Greta Bridge way where helpless youth is starved and oppressed by rapacious masters, and there is a mission for him to fulfil. He is with rollicking companions, and they sit down to a prodigious breakfast—'a piece of beef about the size and much the shape of my portmanteau, tea or coffee, ham and eggs'. He does not say he partook of them all, but at the end of the catalogue laconically remarks, 'We are now going to look about it.' He looked about it and found the Academy for Young Gentlemen; he went as far as Boroughbridge, and saw an empty barn by the roadside where his hero Nicholas was one morning to find the fugitive Smike.

The complete story of the visit to Bowes and Dotheboys Hall is told first-hand in the Preface to the novel thus originating, though it is by no means certain that Dickens selected the worst or even the real offender for his pillory; and Shaw, the prototype of Squeers, has had ardent vindicators and defenders. Nor must we forget that, if epitaphs sometimes tell the truth, a very warm tribute to the original of Mr. and Miss Squeers may be read on a gravestone in the churchyard. But Yorkshire schools themselves deserved the evil reputation they had earned, and their exposure and destruction were justified and laudable. With the help of Charles Smithson, of Easthorpe Hall, Malton, partner of Dickens's old schoolfellow, Thomas Mitton, a pious fraud was concocted concerning a supposititious little boy for whom search was to be made. He met the original of John Browdie, a farmer of Broadiswood, or, as some say, a Yorkshire attorney. It does not much matter now. He secured essential facts, and he saw in Bowes churchyard on a dreary winter afternoon the inscription that George Ashton Taylor, aged nineteen, had 'died suddenly at Mr. William Shaw's Academy, 1822'. Dickens's imagination at once conjured up a lad whose heart had been broken. 'Depend upon it,' he wrote in furious indignation, 'that the rascalities of those Yorkshire schoolmasters cannot easily be exaggerated.'

So we start with Nicholas from the 'Saracen's Head', Snow Hill, clamber up a coach, hear the stout old Yorkshireman of a guard blow his horn till he is out of breath, dine at Eton-Slocombe, canter on to Grantham, and, if there be a breakdown, while away the time by listening to the story of the five Sisters of York. Dickens had heard the legend when lunching with Dr. Camidge, the organist at York Minster. And a fine story it makes as related by the grey-haired gentleman who was able to revive the atmosphere of an old-world spot where the five sisters dwelt in an old-fashioned house, with overhanging gables and balconies of rudely carved oak, standing within a pleasant orchard, surrounded by a rough stone wall, whence a stout archer might have winged an arrow to St. Mary's Abbey.

'The old Abbey flourished then,' said the grey-haired gentleman, 'and the five sisters, living on its fair domains, paid yearly dues to the black monks of Saint Benedict, to which fraternity it belonged.' It is a tale of the time of Henry IV, of bright maidens and a moody monk, of changing fortunes, and of one sister who passed away—'in the minster nave was one flat stone beneath which she slept in peace'. And because she had loved light and colour in her life, she who was now in eternal shadow, the four sisters caused to be executed in five large compartments of richly stained glass a faithful copy of the embroidery work on which they had been engaged when the monk first saw them and rebuked their worldliness. The five compartments were fitted into one large window through which the sun shone brightly, 'and throwing a stream of brilliant light upon the pavement fell warmly on the name of Alice'. In time there were five names for the sun to illumine, and the window came to bear the name of Five Sisters. Such the legend, and it haunted the broken dreams of one listener until the coach arrived, and he could rest a while at the 'George and New Inn' in the village now known as Thorpe Grange.

This was not to be the end of Dickens's experiences in Yorkshire, but times and customs changed, and the railway next bore him to the towns where audiences thronged to hear his voice. He spent a December day in 1847 at the Mechanics' Institution, Leeds, and met George Stephenson; but Leeds depressed him, and ten years later, when he took part in writing the *Lazy Tour of Two Idle Apprentices*, he recalled his arrival at the railway station—with 'a little rotten platform (converted into artificial torchwood by smoke and ashes)', and he spoke of the 'branchless woods of vague black chimneys of the manufacturing bosom of Yorkshire'. The towns, he said, looked in the cinderous net 'as though they had one and all been on fire and were just put out'. Leeds he 'particularly detested as an odious place'; he was there when it was 'recovering from the double excitement of the Festival and the Queen', and the streets looked 'like a great circus with the season just finished. All sorts of garish triumphal arches were put up for the Queen, and they have got smoky, and have been looked out of countenance by the sun, and are blistered and patchy, and half up and half down, and are hideous to behold.'

Proceeding with his travels the following year, Dickens reached Sheffield and received a tumultuous welcome; the episode that touched him most was that when he read the *Carol* and of Tiny Tim who 'did *not* die', the demonstrative Yorkshiremen received the words 'with a most prodigious shout and roll of thunder'. He went to Hull, and gave a whimsical account of his friends in the excitement of the night being tousled, turned upside down, their shirt-fronts and their waistcoats torn off; and then his peregrinations took him to Halifax—'as horrible a place as I ever saw'. But he was charmed with Whitby—'the queerest place, with the strangest people in it, leading the oddest lives of dancing, newspaper reading, and *tables d'hôte*'. An inn struck his fancy because it was up a back-yard, and oyster-shell grottoes were the only view from the best private room. Harrogate had his attention, and then he had to make his way to

Scarborough, but trains did not run on Sundays (this was in 1858)—'the piety of York obliging us to leave at six this morning, and we had to engage a special engine'. The journey enabled him to attend the funeral of his friend Smithson, at Malton Abbey. Not only had he helped Dickens in his *Nickleby* inquiries, but he had found him a 'gifted raven' to replace the precious Grip. Whilst at Easthorpe Hall, preparing the Gamp chapters in *Martin Chuzzlewit*, Dickens had written: 'O heaven! Such green woods as I was rambling along down in Yorkshire last July! For days and weeks we never saw the sky but through green boughs; and all day long I cantered over such soft moss and turf that the horse's feet scarcely made a sound upon it!' And a year later the friend—'one of the jolliest of the jolly, keeping a big old country house, with an ale cellar something larger than a reasonable church'—was dead at the early age of nine-and-thirty.

Of all the Yorkshire resorts it was Doncaster that excited a certain bitterness of feeling, not so much because of the place itself as because of its associations and of the gambling crowd which infested it on occasion. He stayed at the 'Angel' with Wilkie Collins, who, being incapacitated by a badly strained leg, was at that period 'the only individual in Doncaster who stands by the brink of the full-flowing stream, and is not swept away by it in common with all the rest of the species'. For the St. Leger was being run, and Dickens wrote of the crowd in one of the most caustic and unequivocal chapters that he ever penned. Not only the visible horrors, but the ghost of invisible horror, Palmer, the man who poisoned his betting companion, haunted him throughout the visit. It cannot be said in the main that Dickens's Yorkshire experiences were happy. But he lived long enough to see a mighty change for the better in one respect, and he made a curious avowal in a Christmas sketch when referring to the coming of the railway: 'In common with other people I occasionally affect to lament the passing of the stage-coach, which everybody dreaded as a serious penance then.' With such words Dickens says farewell to the Great North Road.

Another voice of the earlier times reaches us. A burly fellow, well bewigged, is jogging along in surly mood, and, zounds, sir! he means to tell you what he thinks about things, and he will talk to you of oats and wheat, and peasants and poverty, and you shall hear him whether you like it or not, and, egad, sir! you shall read it, too, in his famous *Register*. For it is none other than William Cobbett, always in a rage—or nearly always; for, after all, there was one memorable day when he reached Leeds, that 'fine and opulent capital, for the capital it is', and had so fine a reception that he forthwith forgot all his wrath, 'and what I set the highest value on is, that I find I produced a prodigious effect in that important town!'

Time passes, and we are in the decorous days of the good Queen somewhere in the 'sixties. A lady, sombrely clad, with a heavy face lit up by expressive eyes, has found her way along the Great North Road. She leans upon the arm of an ugly side-whiskered man who talks volubly, and talks well, for with all his faults George Lewes is a man of learning and George Eliot understands and loves him. In place of the bustle and din and jollity of the old scenes we now have a sedate record of a visit to Leeds where 'we were received by Dr. Clifford Allbutt with whom we stayed till the middle of the day on Wednesday. Then we went by train to Ilkley, and from thence took carriage to Bolton.' Can we trace a little growing excitement in the announcement that 'the weather had been grey for two days, but on this evening the sun shone out, and we had a delightful stroll before dinner, getting our first view of the Priory'? Or in this: 'On Thursday we spent the whole day in rambling through the woods to Barden Tower and back. Our comfortable little inn was the Red Lion, and we were tempted to lengthen our stay. But on Friday morning the sky was threatening, so we started for Newark, which we had visited in old days on our expedition to Gainsborough. At Newark we found our old inn, the Ram, opposite the ruins of the castle, and then we went for a stroll along the banks of the Trent, seeing some charming quiet landscapes'—written by the same hand that quivered with passion as it penned the story of Maggie Tulliver!

So they come and go, this medley retinue of wanderers along the Great North Road, scampering or sauntering, galloping or idling, some with a loud 'Yoho!' some in meditative silence, some to war and some to prayer. We watch them through the centuries. And there was one, not far from our own times, who made his way along that highway to find peace and silence among the Yorkshire hills, and to comprehend nature's freedom and beauty: 'Peace at last; no roll of cart-wheel, nor mutter of sullen voices in the back shop; but curlew cry in space of heaven, and welling of bell-toned streamlet by its shadowy rock. Freedom at last! Far as foot or eye can race or range, the moor and cloud. Loneliness at last, among these deserted vales. Pride of purple rocks, and river pools of blue, and tender wilderness of glittering trees, and misty light of evening on immeasurable hills.' So Turner became a painter of the strength of nature and of the labour and sorrow of men, 'the great human truth made visible,' and it was the Great North Road that led him forward toward the goal.

CHAPTER III

THE WHITE-WALLED CAPITAL

STATELY, venerable, bearing its hoary age with serenity, York is very old, and does not conceal the fact but glories in it. Her many centuries are not a burden but an honour, and she confronts the age with dignity and strength. Should ever Time run back to fetch the age of gold, York might be the starting-place.

There was a traveller from a far country years ago who from the summit of the central tower of the Minster viewed the country round, and found one word forced to his lips—'Blessèd!' He had made the ascent on a day when there was brilliant sunshine but a keen wind, and the storm-clouds were streaming away before the blast. Far beneath were seen the red roofs of the houses, the grey churches, the devious lanes, the circling walls, and the silver thread of the Ouse. As far as eye could reach stretched forth 'a smiling landscape of emerald meadow and cultivated field: here a patch of woodland, and there a silver gleam of water; here a manor-house nestled amid stately trees, and there an ivy-covered fragment of ruined masonry; and everywhere the green lines of the flowering hedge'. While he lingered and meditated the muffled thunder of the organ rose, rolling and throbbing, and seemed to shake the great tower as with a mighty sound of jubilation and worship. 'Those old monks,' he said, 'who built the abbeys of Britain, laid their foundations not alone deeply in the earth, but deeply in the human soul.' And then he repeated his devout word.

The history of York stretches back so far that it thins away into myth. Geoffrey of Monmouth peering into the twilight thought he saw the great stature and prodigious strength of a figure named Ebraucus, a ruler for fifty years who built a stronghold—and called it from his own name Kaerebrauc. This happened, he helpfully adds, 'about the time that David reigned in Judaea'. As an alternative, in case of doubt, there is the story of a Saxon Duke of Effroe who was drowned in the river and the spot was commemorated by his name. To the Romans, when they came, it was Evora or Ebora, the town on the Eure, and hence Ebora-vicum and the contraction Eboracum. Richard of Cirencester, starting on more definite lines, told of the Roman colony called Sexta from its being the station of the victorious Sixth Legion, and 'afterwards distinguished by the presence of many emperors, and raised to the privileges of a municipal city', that is, granted all the rights of Roman citizenship, the highest attainable class of honour.

What we know for fact of this classic, and, in part, consecrated ground, is that Constantine the Great, the conquering Caesar, master of the known world, was here invested with the imperial purple. There is no description of that momentous event, and it is left to the imagination to picture the solemn ceremonial and the assembly of the Legions, while the roar of 'Ave, Caesar!' echoed through the air. But the Victorious Legion was not left untroubled. Besieged by Scots and Britons under a Scythian leader in the reign of Severus, the aged emperor drove them off and with his cohorts marched into the Lowlands where, Roman fashion, he seized the business opportunity to make roads and drain the marshes, the whole expedition costing him fifty thousand men. A later revolt would have been put down mercilessly, but Severus was stricken at York, leaving the government to Geta the dog and Caracalla the wolf. 'Cherish the Legions,' he bade them. Then, calling for the golden urn which was to contain his ashes, he said almost in the vein of Ecclesiasticus, 'I have been all, and am no better for it. This urn will soon hold what the whole world could not contain,' and presently on a pile of wood on a hill near Holgate imperial Caesar's corpse was turned to dust. The deadly feuds which followed between the two successors enter into Roman history, but York witnessed much of the slaughter.

Scandinavian rovers descended by sea on the Yorkshire coast, pirating and burning, and quaffing the good ale so much to their liking; the tumultuous Danes came with their blood-red banners streaming from snake-headed ships, and discovered the slow-moving river which led them to that white-walled castrum where Rome had set the foundations of an empire. The vagaries of the York byways are attributed to these half-savage invaders, who found a four-square town, and, indifferent architects, lacking logic and design, did their rebuilding in crooked and haphazard style, and made their Goodramgate and Fossgate, leaving the real gates to be termed 'bars'—some in their simpler courts and squares now dignified with Georgian mansions. Saunter minsterwards towards Bootham, and from the Northern Port glance backward at the bar and the towers, and the finest Gothic combination that our land affords will be viewed.

The history of York definitely changed on an Easter Day in the year 627, when King Edwin was baptized, and as proof of his Christian faith decided to build a large and noble church of stone. This was the first Minster, and Paulinus was the first archbishop. But six years later the king was slain at Hatfield, and Oswald the saint succeeded him; Penda, the Mercian pagan, was finally routed at 'the county of Loidis', otherwise Leeds; monasteries and abbeys sprang up, including one at Whitby which served as Edwin's shrine, and the Faith was triumphantly established in the north.

The Middle Ages lurk in York's thoroughfares. From a raised seat on the Wall opposite the antique Treasurer's House you see the dominating outline of the Minster in all its magnificence carved against the sky. You look down and note the quaint houses where each of the upper stories overhangs the one below, nodding companionably the one to the other so that cronies could almost shake hands across the street. Names have the tang and flavour of far-away days, and the many Gates (which make quite a catalogue) suggest at once origin and use, and there is even a roll of melody in them—Spurriergate, Colliergate, Micklegate, Walmgate, Stonegate, High Petergate, High Ousegate, Jubbergate, Sunigate, Fossgate, and Goodramgate. Of course an ancient city has it Shambles and Butchers' Quarter; Stonebow Lane is obviously reminiscent; the spirit of antic humour mocks us in Whipma-Whopma Gate, where felons were flogged in the good old days; while Mucky Peg Lane, if not a corruption, may give dubious fame to an inglorious slattern. A bewildering feature of the streets, rows, and alleys is that they lead nowhere in particular, and apparently carry out a jester's whim of bringing the wanderer unexpectedly back to his starting-place. They serve one useful purpose in permitting an intimate study of the habitations of a bygone generation, each with its own stamp. The spectator is surprised to

THE GABLES OF OLD YORK

find how 'the grey and mouldering remnants of the feudal age are blent with the structures of the democratic present'; and is struck with modern objects consorting so anomalously with donjon, barbican, drawbridge, portcullis, and moat. The narrow streets, the brick buildings of low stature splashed with red tiles, and the cincture of the massive Walls with their bastions, slit-holes, and gates, make a picture almost without parallel; but there are additions to render it peculiarly fantastic—here, an Elizabethan house, with overhanging timber-crossed fronts and peaked gables, bearing proudly its date of 1574; there, a quadrangular court with carved gateway and bright with red timber, centuries old, and not vainly boasting that the Neville family were the builders. It is now the Clergy House, and was once St. William's College, one of the two institutions (the other, the Bedern, is long since gone) established in the times of discipline for those priests who were a little froward and rather prone to substitute dagger for cross. Thoughts of days of daring are evoked as we stand before the doorway over which the inscription runs, 'Dieu nous donne bonne aventure,' and we find we are at the hall of the Merchant Adventurers, and can take a glance at the stout oak beams within, the rich panellings, and the many relics of the thriving days of the trade guilds. Once a year the Merchant Adventurers, for the guild survives, make their way in all the glory of the ancient costume to the underground chapel, and there a service is held. The interior has been converted into an impressive show-place, and a lady of learning—upon whom the dignity of the guild has been worthily conferred—tells the story with knowledge and enthusiasm. A portion, of this unique building was once a Sunday school, and the felicitous association of gain and goodness was later exemplified by a Penny Bank in the corner.

If York City is thick inlaid with the treasures of ages, we may also find a little gold-dust of romance in its byways. A handful can be gathered from Wilkie Collins's *No Name*, the heroine of which, Margaret Vanstone, finds a refuge in the narrow street of Skeldergate. Describing it in the 'forties, Collins referred to the few old houses then left as being 'disguised in melancholy modern costume of white-wash and cement-shops of the smaller and poorer order, intermixed here and there with dingy ware-houses and joyless private residences of red brick'. On the riverside, he said, the houses were separated at intervals by lanes running down to the water, and disclosing little plots of open ground, with the masts of sailing barges rising beyond. Then the street ceased on a sudden, and the broad flow of the Ouse, the trees, the meadows, the public walk on one bank and the towing-path on the other, were open to view. But 'the quietest place in York' was the walk on the Walls, and the novelist chose it for a momentous interview between Margaret and the amiable rogue, Captain Wragge. It was appropriate enough for the dramatic purpose; on one hand stretched the open country beyond the Walls—'The rich green meadows, the boundary trees dividing them, the broad windings of the river in the distance, the scattered buildings nearer to view; all wrapped in the evening stillness, all made beautiful by the evening peace'; and on the other hand 'the majestic west front of York Minster soared over the city, and caught the last brightest light of heaven on the summits of its lofty towers.'

So, as is the way of the York streets, we return to

our starting-place once more. But if it so happen, when we at last depart, our path leads toward the former forest of Galtres, we shall only read with amused interest the olden record that it was once the custom for armed men stationed at Bootham Bar to keep watch, and to accompany pilgrims some part of the journey lest they be assailed by thieves or devoured by wolves. In these days a traveller casts aside all thought of ancient peril and pain, and with a comfort Caesar never knew starts out from the most praised railway station in the kingdom.

Of the Castle, grim and gloomy as such strongholds were meant to be, one story has to be told so much of shame and terror that we wish it could be classed among the legends ; but it is a hard truth of the hard twelfth century of fanaticism. The Jews in that period of war and want, according to one of the least-bigoted historians, William of Newburgh, were extortioners who enjoyed the luxury and pomp of kings—*cultu fastuque poene regis provedentes.* But Isaac D'Israeli, writing with sympathy for the race to which he belonged, gives a moving account of the poignant event which occurred within the Castle in 1190. Richard of the Lion Heart was on the throne. The Jews sought his protection, but the superstitious multitude, suspecting witchcraft, ejected them from Westminster Abbey when they attended the coronation, and in a panic the ostracized people fled. Benedict, a Jew of York, allowed himself to be baptized in hope of saving his life, and with his rich friend Jocenus made his way back to the city, where he died of his wounds.

The apostate had not been forgotten ; the Jews of York attacked his house but only found his corpse ; alarmed by reprisals they turned to Jocenus, who prevailed on the governor of the castle to provide them with an asylum. Five hundred or more betook themselves thither with their possessions. Then the rabble broke loose, and, vowing vengeance, burned and sacked the Jewish habitations. Little of the wealth they expected to find was in their reach. The fury increased. The Jews inside the castle lost trust in the governor, and after one of his excursions refused him admission. The sheriff sent the soldiery. The people, many of them in debt to the usurers, gleefully joined in the attack. A priest fanned the flames with his adjurations that the enemies of Christ must be destroyed. Soon it was clear that the besieged could not hold out.

Their leader, or Rabbin, a man of learning and of heroic spirit, realized the desperate situation, called a council, and delivered an address to the men of Israel which, if rhetorical, touches upon sublimity. It begins with the philosophy of the mystic, the fatalist, the man of unswerving faith, that none can question the wisdom of the God of their ancestors, and that if the command has gone forth to die for His law, none must ask why. The Law had been preserved pure through the Captivity, eternal hope depended upon it, and what could be done less than to die for it ? Then the Rabbin uttered his words of awe : 'If we fall into the hands of our enemies our death will be ignominious and cruel. We must elude their tortures. We ourselves should be our executioners. Let us voluntarily surrender our lives to our Creator. We trace the invisible Jehovah in His acts. God calls for us ; let us be not unworthy of that call. So I advise, men of Israel,' A few demurred and stood aside ; the majority approved.

All the goods were burnt, all the valuables destroyed.

Then every husband slew his wife, every father his children ; this done, the men turned their blades upon themselves. At last only Jocenus and the Rabbin remained. 'Jocenus, being the chief Jew, was distinguished by the last mark of human respect, in receiving his death from the consecrated hand of the Rabbin, who immediately after performed the melancholy duty on himself.' Then the people broke in, only to gaze upon five hundred corpses and upon walls consumed by fire. They killed the few who had shrunk from taking their own lives, and the extermination of the Jews of York was complete. D'Israeli has found in the obscure Rabbin a worthy companion of the illustrious Cato.

The castle history in later days was darkened with many tragedies, and Clifford's Tower and Micklegate Bar became names of dread import. Shakespeare has painted in words, as Rembrandt would have done in harsh colour, the last tragic scenes of the Wars of the Roses. The Duke of York in Sandal Castle with six thousand men was beleaguered by three times that number under the Duke of Somerset. He was entreated by Sir David Hale, a faithful old counsellor, not to venture out until reinforcements came ; but his own arrogance and Queen Margaret's taunts led him to decide 'to fight mine enemies though I fight them alone'. Out he sallied. Wakefield saw the issue, and heads were spiked on Micklegate Bar.

It is with a weary iteration that we hear of these happenings at the so-called Traitors' Gate. Heads, whether of dukes or commoners, so long as they were those of men on the losing side, were to be seen impaled as hideous warnings. Now it was White Rose or Red Rose, now Papist or Protestant, now Cavalier or

Roundhead, now Jacobite or Hanoverian; fate was settled by the arbitrament of the sword, and Micklegate Bar furnished the evidence. Two of the last of the heads to be seen there were of Jacobites, and it is declared they exhibited their ghastliness for eight years. Then they were stolen, and after a reward had been offered the culprit was found to be a poor little tailor, who went to prison for his 'unlawful and audacious action'.

The head of an Archbishop of York, Richard Scrope, was among those to be seen on the city walls. He was an adherent of the Earl of March, and involved in the conspiracy against Henry IV. Chief Justice Gascoigne was directed to condemn him forthwith, but refused; a court creature was more amenable. On June 8th 1405 the Archbishop, according to the historian Gent, was 'put upon a horse, about the value of forty pence, with a halter about its neck, but without a saddle on its back. And the Archbishop gave thanks to God, saying, "I never liked a horse better than I like this". Twice he sang the Psalm *Exaudi*, being habited in a sky-coloured loose garment, with sleeves of the same colour, but they would not permit him to wear the linen vesture used by bishops. At the place of execution (a field between Bishopthorpe and York) he laid his hood and tunic on the ground, offered himself and his cause to heaven, and desired the executioner to give him five strokes in token of the five wounds of our Saviour, which was done accordingly.' Such men knew how to die.

After Wakefield, on the last day of 1460, when the Duke of York was slain, his head crowned with a mock diadem of paper, was spiked, his face turned to the city, and the taunt was made: 'So York may overlook the town of York.' A dozen other noble heads were placed there also, 'for a spectacle to the people and a terror to adversaries', but fortune was reversed on Towton Field, by the Duke's son, the Earl of March, and Shakespeare gives us the command of Warwick—

> From off the gates of York fetch down the head,
> Your father's head, which Clifford placèd there;
> Instead thereof, let this supply the room;
> Measure for measure must be answerèd.

And the heads of the Earl of Devonshire, the Earl of Kyme, Sir William Hill, and Sir Thomas Foulford replaced the Duke's.

Another figure appears, and we glimpse the wistful face of Mary Queen of Scots. A conference at York under the presidency of the Duke of Norfolk reviewed the acts of the rebellious northern lords who supported her; the production of the forged Casket Letters deepened the suspicion of the hapless queen's guilt and danger. Two years later, so fervent were the northerners in their devotion to the Catholic cause, that the Earl of Sussex wrote to Queen Elizabeth, 'There were not ten gentlemen in Yorkshire that did allow her proceedings in the cause of religion,' and Mary was promptly removed to a less zealous part of the kingdom. The last attempt to restore Papal power in England by means of arms was made when the Earl of Northumberland fought desperately to dethrone Queen Elizabeth. Obdurate to the last, he avowed the Pope's supremacy, denied subjection to the queen, affirmed the land to be in a schism, and her obedient subjects little better than heretics, and his handsome, silver-haired head was soon afterwards to be seen spiked on Micklegate Bar.

It is a relief to turn to the lighter and happier passages in York's history, and to the men who laboured for peace and who helped on progress. One vision that flashes upon us from the far past is that of a scholar-priest, Alcuin or Albinus by name, born in the eighth century, and becoming the adviser and confidant of the mighty Charlemagne himself. Educated at the cloister-school, and at the age of twenty-three becoming the master, he so made his intellectual force felt that he was chosen to conduct the education of the emperor's family, and it is said that at the court at Aix-la-Chapelle the monarch deigned to sit at his feet as a pupil. His fame is as an apostle of culture in a dark and barbarous time; writing much, engaging in theological controversy, leaving many a commentary, treatise, and biography for posterity, he breathed out a potent inspiration which animated the ages, quickened the desire for knowledge, and helped on the Renaissance which revived the stagnant minds of men. The revival was continued in other form by Hugo Goes, who, only five-and-twenty years after Caxton had set up his press in Westminster, introduced printing into Yorkshire in the minster yard. Learning was fostered, and the county produced scholars like Roger Ascham, Miles Coverdale, and Bishop Alcock; and famous grammar schools were reared at York, Hull, Sedbergh, and Giggleswick.

Of York's supreme jewel, the Minster, so much should be said that volumes alone would be adequate. A few relics remain of the Saxon foundation: a piece of herring-bone wall, a fragment of stone staircase. The Norman period is represented by four clustered columns. Two hundred years went to the making of the glorious fane, the loftiest of all English cathedrals. Between 1227 and 1412 Archbishops Grey, John le Romaine, de Melton, Thoresby, and Walter Skirlow, Bishop of Durham, carried on the work of construction.

THE FIVE SISTERS WINDOW, YORK MINSTER

Its east window, the artistic glory of the interior, was the work of John Thornton of Coventry, who was commissioned to complete the work in three years, and his payment was four shillings a day, with a yearly addition of five pounds and a bonus of ten when the work was satisfactorily finished. So he wrought and produced his masterpiece, seventy-five feet in height and thirty-two in width, divided into nine lights, and with a hundred compartments picturing scenes from the Old Testament and the Book of Revelations. Thanks to Fairfax during the Civil War the original glass has been preserved; it is said that he had it taken out and buried. We may still see it in gracious evening beauty when the rising moon, 'as she gleams through the dripping clouds, pours silver rays upon it, and all the Bible stories told there in such exquisite hues and forms glow with heavenly lustre on the dark vista of chancel and nave'; and we can behold it in glowing splendour when morning comes and 'the first beams of the rising sun stream through the great casement, and illumine the figures of saints and archbishops, and gild the old tattered battle-flags in the chancel aisle, and touch with blessing the marble effigies of the dead'.

To tradition associated with the holy place only one slight reference can be made, as perhaps the most remarkable and ancient—the bearing to the high altar on Christmas Eve of mistletoe, even as the Druids had done in their temples; and the proclaiming of universal liberty, pardon for offenders, and freedom vouched to 'all sorts of inferior and even wicked people at the gates of the city towards the four quarters of the heaven'. To the relics, also, only one reference can be permitted, and it is to the ivory drinking-horn of Ulphus the Dane, who, after the dispute between his sons, rode to York, filled the horn with wine, and before the altar bestowed all his lands and wealth upon the Church. And as we turn reluctantly away from the glorious fane we may hear, from the neighbouring tower of St. Michael's, curfew tolling as it has done since the days of the Conqueror.

CHAPTER IV

TURRETS AND STANDARDS

ON his tour through England the philosophic Emerson remarked that 'castles are proud things but 'tis safest to be outside them'. Their ruins to-day, however pathetic, are more agreeable to gaze upon than would have been their former menacing strength. Many a Yorkshire fortress looms up in a battle-region, and is a grim reminder of times when history had its turning-points. Dynasties were changed, as at Stamford Bridge, where Harold's slaughter of the Danes seemed to assure Saxon ascendancy; but nine days later he was dead at Hastings. The Yorkshiremen remained true to him and his cause, and were among the last to yield to the conquering Norman: not till their land had been laid waste (Domesday Book records how thoroughly) did they sullenly submit. Lisle Bowles in his poem on the 'Last Saxon' tells how William at York was troubled by terrible dreams of the return of Harold's hosts; but there was an effective method of keeping enemies in check.

The Normans were builders, and believed in strong walls and lofty towers; twenty castles rose like ramparts, and served not only as strongholds for the feudal lords, but as defences against the encroaching Scots. Nature accorded Richmond her handsome position, and William the Conqueror gave Richmond to Alan of Brittany. This Conqueror's favourite quickly seized upon the promontory jutting over the Swale as site for a castle rather than tamely accept the less proudly situated stronghold at Gilling, near by, from which he had ousted its Saxon lord. But this strong castle had never owners strong enough to keep it, and though Alan of Brittany received with the castle more manors than he could visit in a month there was not an odd acre of land to go with it by the time of Charles II. It has its legends of King Arthur and his sleeping knights, and of the drummer boy who sought a way to Easeby Abbey, never returned, but still sends a muffled roll above the melancholy sing-song of the Swale; but a surer story is that William the Lion, King of Scotland, was held fast by the castle's strength, and yielded his pride in swearing allegiance to his rival. And one other figure haunts the chambers—the Lady Constance, who with her little son and daughter was held captive by King John:

> Here I and sorrow sit,
> Here is my throne, bid Kings come bow to it.

Alan the Red at Richmond, Mowbray at Thirsk, Romilles at Skipton, de Lacy at Pontefract, Warenne at Sandal and Conisborough, were men of doughty deeds which rang in song; and as they grew in power they struck for or against their king according to interest or mood and turned the tide of surging conflict. The name of the Scropes, at their great fourfold stronghold, Bolton Castle, which took twenty years to build in the fourteenth century, once exercised terror far and near through the county. At Boroughbridge the barons pitted their strength against Edward II, and lost; the Earl of Hereford was slain on the bridge, and the leader, the Earl of Lancaster, was pursued, overtaken, and lost his head. Thirty of the barons and knights suffered at York, and for three years their

RICHMOND, THE CASTLE WALK

4

bodies in chains made a fearsome warning to rebels. One gallant soldier in this battle won an earldom; the king made him Earl of Carlisle. It was a short-lived glory. At Byland Abbey, where the advancing Scots routed an English force, the new earl was indicted for collusion with the enemy, and his sentence was: 'To be degraded both himself and his heirs from the rank of earl, to be ungirt of his sword, his gilded spurs to be hacked from his heels, to be hanged, drawn, and beheaded, his heart and entrails torn out and burnt to ashes, and the ashes scattered to the winds; his carcase to be divided into four quarters, and his head to be spiked on London Bridge.' The awful doom could not shake the heart of the old warrior. 'Divide my body as you please,' said he, 'but I give my soul to God.'

At Pontefract a feeble Plantagenet vanished in mysterious tragedy to make way for bold Bolingbroke. In York desperate Queen Margaret waited on Palm Sunday with tremulous anxiety for the issue of the fierce contest at Towton which meant the holding or the loss of a crown, and though heroes fought and fell for her son, and chivalrous Warwick slew his horse rather than have an advantage over the common soldier, the battle in the snow spelt ruin for the Lancastrian cause and the Red Rose. Henry went to his obscure fate, and Edward was crowned in York's fane. The fury and revenges of that battle in which chivalry had no part may be read in a poet's lines:

From the gracious Minster-towers
Of York the priests behold afar
The field of Towton shimmer like a star
With light of lance and helm; while both the powers
Misnamed from the fair rose, with one fell blow,
In snow-dazed, blinding air
Mass'd on the burnside bare,
Each army, as one man, drove at the opposing foe.

Ne'er since then, and ne'er before,
On England's fields with English hands
Have met for death such myriad myriad bands,
Such wolf-like fury, and such greed of gore:
No natural kindly touch, no check of shame:
And no such bestial rage
Blots our long story's page;
Such lewd remorseless swords, such selfishness of aim.

. . . . .

Evening falls, and from the Minster height
They see the wan Ouse stream
Blood-dark with slaughter gleam
And hear the demon-struggle shrieking through the night.

Middleham, now in ruin, played a big part in tumultuous times, for it was the citadel of Warwick the King-maker, with almost sovereign power of his own, living in mighty state in the moors. 'To this lonely fortalice,' as one historian puts it, 'he consigned the long-haired handsome Edward, soldier and voluptuary, leader at the wassail, victor in the field.' And when Barnet had been fought, Crookback Gloucester made his home within the gaunt walls, brought there the Lady Anne, and saw the birth of a son who lived but a few weeks. The memory of King Richard was so strong in the north, wrote Bacon in his graphic style, that 'it lay like lees in the bottom of men's hearts, and if the vessel was stirred it would come up'. The now roofless rooms of the castle witnessed alike the purest waves of joy and the deepest waves of sorrow that ever beat against the soul of Crookback. Much that is legendary has fastened upon this stirring figure, and moving now among these deserted remnants of a castle where, 'standing on the top of happy hours', he held Court and exercised kingship, the mind leaps away

MIDDLEHAM

to Bosworth and knows that Richard will ride no more through this castle gateway. 'Saddle White Windsor for the field to-morrow,' echoes with sinister sound from the king's tent and vibrates around this frowning keep. But the unanswered shout, 'A horse, a horse,' cuts the air with its clangour and the flag on Middleham Castle droops. Look forward a little to the career of Mary Queen of Scots. The king who lost his life at Bosworth had thirty-two years before been born at Fotheringay, where a queen was to die. But here she comes now, at full gallop, breathing the happy air of freedom! By the scheming and daring of young Christopher Norton she had evaded her jailers at Bolton Castle, and rode out with her worshipping escort, only, alas, to be overtaken. There are perils of course in the picture, because it is contended that the queen never rode so far from Bolton Castle, and never gladdened for so long the daring heart of her would-be deliverer. So, 'tread softly, for you tread on dreams!'

The narrative takes other form with that pitiful episode, the Pilgrimage of Grace. The march of the devotees of the Old Faith began in Lincolnshire and ended in Lancashire, and the intermediate county had its share of suffering when the leader, Robert Aske, matched religious fervour against the arms of ruthless battalions. At Bawtry, King Henry was met by two hundred Yorkshire gentlemen clad in velvet, and four thousand tall yeomen and serving-men; on their knees they made submission through their spokesman, Sir Robert Bowes, and would have placated him with a gift of nine hundred pounds. It was in vain, as the gibbets were soon to show. On Doncaster bridge, after a conference between Aske and the noblemen who opposed the anti-Papal policy of the king, the banner of St. Cuthbert was hoisted and they marched to their doom. No mercy to the 'wilful gentlemen', either high or low, was to be shown. Abbots and friars, lords and commoners, suffered alike in the luckless crusade, and the Duke of Norfolk in callous terms reported to his sovereign that Sir Robert Constable of Flamborough had been hanged above the highest gate of the town and been 'so trimmed in chains that I think his bones will hang there this hundred years'. A short way with dissenters in the days of Bluff King Hal.

Another tragic 'Rising' in the time of Queen Bess imparts a grim fascination to moated and battlemented Markenfield Hall. That meeting-place of warriors presented a strange scene when men gathered around the young lord, each bearing on his breast a crucifix, and ready to march under a banner emblazoned with the five wounds of Christ. The standard-bearer was Richard Norton, High Sheriff of Yorkshire, father of eleven sons and eight daughters, ready to stake everything for religion. Heavy was the penalty this family endured when the 'Rising' was suppressed. Like Thomas Markenfield, Norton fled abroad, and both died in poverty. Two of Norton's sons were executed; seven in all were condemned. They petitioned for their lives, their property was seized, and in the ruthless manner of old times their supporters were hanged in every town and village round about. The old stone hall is haunted by these mournful memories, and they suggested a theme for Wordsworth, the story of Francis Norton and the consecrated maid, Emily, and the coming of the White Doe:

> When the bells of Rylstone played
> Their Sabbath music—'God us ayde'.

The crucial Yorkshire battle was at Marston Moor, where Prince Rupert by his recklessness and Cromwell by his strategy brought to ruin the hopes of the Cavaliers. The Civil War had raged with fluctuating fortunes. In Yorkshire King Charles had high hopes of success, but the gates of Hull were closed against him by order of the governor, and he lost the best magazine of munitions of war; had it been at the disposal of the Royalists the course of the disastrous struggle might have been diverted. That episode is described in quaint and pithy terms by Colonel Hutchinson's wife: 'Now had the King raised an army of three thousand foot and one thousand horse, with which he went to Beverley, in order to besiege Hull. When he was within two hours' march of the place, Sir John Hotham floated the county about it, and Sir John Meldrum, sallying out of the town, with five hundred townsmen, made the King's party retreat to Beverley. But they beleaguered the town, into which the Parliament sent a relief of five hundred men, by water, with whom Meldrum made another rally, routed the leaguer-soldiers, killed some, made others prisoners, took the magazine of arms and ammunitions, which was in a barn, with their fire-balls, and fired the barn. Thereupon the King's council of war broke up the siege, from whence the King went back to York.' Hotham's bold decision had been of supreme importance, and he expected good reward. But Fairfax seized the generalship of the north, and Hotham, grievously offended, gave service to the king whom he had formerly thwarted. Now he would have delivered Hull into his hands, but the plot failed; and, arrested by his own nephew at Beverley, he was beheaded as a traitor on Tower Hill.

Marston Moor was gloriously won and irretrievably

lost. The Cavaliers first drove the men of sword and Bible in headlong rout from the field, and for a few hours King Charles was re-established ; the news sped to him, and bonfires blazed and joy-bells pealed. He heard a few hours later how Cromwell with troops in reserve had fallen upon the victors :

> When 'gainst the unwisely guided King
> The dark self-centred Captain stood,
> And law and right and peace went down
> In that red sea of brothers' blood.

Many an unhorsed Sir Nicholas, his steel cap cleft in twain, his good buff jerkin crimsoned with blood, but still waving the silken standard and crying, 'For Church and King, fair gentlemen, spur on and fight it out', suffered the surprise and despair of his life that day when the flight of Rupert was but the warning prelude to the passing of Charles, and before the eyes of scurrying and stricken men swam the vision of a vacant throne and a royal martyr. They had rushed to blows, 'with naught to win and all to lose', and the knell sounded on Marston Moor.

One of the strangest and maddest episodes of the Civil War has Pontefract for its scene. The castle was held by Captain William Paulden for the King, and his comrade-in-arms, Sir Marmaduke Langdale, was a prisoner at Nottingham. General Rainsborough, appointed to the command of the Parliamentary forces, was at Doncaster. Paulden, aided by Cornet Blackburne and Lieutenant Austwick conceived the daring idea of kidnapping Rainsborough and exchanging him for Langdale. With only twenty-two men they left Pontefract secretly, and planned to trap the Roundhead alive. They obtained access to his room on pretence of bearing a letter to him; whilst he was opening it they told him he was their prisoner but they intended no hurt to him. He and his lieutenant were disarmed, taken down the stairway, and ordered to mount a horse and accompany them. So far all had gone well; then the unexpected happened. Rainsborough became aware that he had only four enemies about him; he drew his foot from the stirrup and roared 'To arms!' In a desperate struggle Rainsborough was run through the body and killed. That was exactly what the kidnappers had wished to avoid, as it rendered their scheme futile; to make the irony of events more marked, Langdale, the man to be redeemed, had, unknown to his friends, made his own escape the night before. The whole adventure was frustrated and it brought dire reprisals. The motive of the Royalists was waived aside by the Roundheads, and when Pontefract Castle was taken six of the garrison were excepted from pardon. Governor Morrice and Cornet Blackburne, condemned to death, escaped a while, were recaptured, and executed at York. Lieutenant Austwick and two others, likewise condemned, hid in a sally-port which had been walled up, and eventually got away; and they lived to welcome the restored King, as did Langdale himself for whom so much had been risked.

'Often,' wrote Thomas de Quincey, 'I used to see, after painting upon the blank darkness a sort of rehearsal while waking, a crowd of ladies, and perhaps a festival of dances. And I heard it said, or I said to myself, "These are English ladies from the unhappy times of Charles I. These are the wives and daughters of those who met in peace, and sat at the same tables, and were allied by marriage or by blood; and yet, after a certain day in August 1642, never smiled upon each other again, nor met but on the field of battle; and at Marston Moor cut aside all ties of blood by the cruel sabre, and washed away in blood the memory of ancient friendship.' "

But not all the castles were darkened by the shadows of war, though few escaped. We may wonder what might have been the fate of Ripley, that brown old Tudor structure, once a feudal fortress, had it not been for happy chance. Cromwell had demanded hospitality after Marston Moor, and the Royalist owner gave it grudgingly. We get as odd a picture of times and persons as even an Ainsworth or Thackeray could imagine when the undaunted hostess, Lady Ingilby, met the victorious General with a brace of pistols in her apron-strings, bade him and his comrades-in-arms to conduct themselves like gentlemen, put a watch on them through the night, and grimly informed them on the morrow that it was well they had behaved in a peaceable manner 'or you would not have left this house alive'.

Conventional history tells us that, on the Restoration, Cromwell's corpse was disinterred and contumeliously treated. But history that is not conventional takes a different turn at Newburgh, the home of the Wombwells. There, where the Lord Protector's saddle of crimson velvet, his holster, and his pistols are preserved, it is declared that his body rests. Mary Cromwell, wife of the second Lord Fauconbridge, foreseeing possible revenges, determined that the bones at Westminster should suffer no sacrilege. At dead of night she removed the body from the vault, and substituted another for it. Cromwell's remains were transferred to Newburgh and placed at the head of a flight of steep steps in a narrow chamber of enormous stonework built and cemented into the wall and impenetrable. For centuries this was the secret of the Bellasyse family, a portion of their private history implicitly credited and whispered from generation to generation.

One of the fortresses which suffered heavily for its loyalty was Skipton Castle, its foundations dating back to the days of the Conquest, and the historic home of the Cliffords whose tombs in a splendour of blazonry are a wonder for the sight. The castle offered a bold defiance to the Parliamentarians, and the penalty was devastation. The motto *Désormais* ('Henceforth'), inscribed upon the parapets of the gateway tower, conveys a double significance when we know that this war-shattered stronghold was piously repaired by Lady Anne Clifford, Lady of the Honor of Skipton in Craven, in 1657–8. 'after it had layne ruinous, pulled down and demolished almost to the foundation by the command of the Parliament, because itt had bin a garrison in the then civill warres in England'. The lady found her inspiration in a verse from Isaiah: 'And they that be of thee shall build the old waste places; thou shalt raise up the foundations of many generations; and thou shalt be called the repairer of the breach, the restorer of paths to dwell in.' Imposing and beautiful both in ruin and strength is this restored edifice to-day, high standing in the midst of scenery solemnly and fantastically environed by limestone rocks. Along the hilly roads lies the way to delectable scenes of verdure and tranquillity, and scenes of rugged and broken grandeur.

History is enshrined in the massive stones of the old fortresses, and the old grey walls, like imperishable pages, yield up the still decipherable romances, now dark, now bright, from the bygone ages. The stirring life that was once within those chambers, the roar to which the vaults echoed, the men of fame who once strode the corridors, the fair faces that glanced from the now-shattered windows, are a dream to-day, though they were history in the past and are still inspiration for the poet. One perfect romance remains to beguile us. The vision of the Shepherd Lord slid into Wordsworth's pensive reverie of the *White Doe of Rylstone* and set him musing on Bolton's old monastic tower and on

> The shy recess
> Of Barden's humble quietness,

and he retold a story so strange that it seems to belong to the realm of fantasy rather than truth.

Its beginning has to be sought in the dark times when over and over again Yorkshire was endangered by the marauding Scots, sometimes driven back, sometimes marching on and taking not only the cattle they needed but the women whose husbands they had slain ; sometimes fearlessly fighting hardy soldiers, and sometimes a band of priests, as at Myrton-on-Swale, and never kept at bay until Robert Bruce was dead and Flodden had been fought. The sternest warrior of that time was Black Clifford, who ravaged without mercy and found fierce joy in battle. His deeds gave him a baleful fame, and to be a Clifford was to be accursed. Then the fortunes of York and Lancaster changed and a loyal leader became in turn a hunted rebel. At such a time the wife of a slain Clifford took her infant son for safety to some shepherds at a distance, preserving her secret, and leaving him to grow up as innocent as Florizel, a tender of the flocks, unlearned in books, but with the lore of field and sky and the

BOLTON PRIORY

deep love of nature in his heart. Well might a poet imagine him in his homely grey visited by

> A gracious fairy
> Who loved the Shepherd Lord to meet
> In his wanderings solitary,

and sang to him of beauty and wonder, led him through the enchanted mazes of Craven, and imparted to him secret powers of divination by which he could foresee the fall of Scotland's king.

The time came when another change in fortune made it possible for the shepherd to return to his rightful place. He sought his home at Barden, he made himself the humble pupil of the learned monks, and he stored in his mind the wisdom that nature had brought him. The people loved the gentle hermit, but deemed him to be a wizard dabbling in forbidden arts. He had no love of pomp or courtly state, or even of company save of the fraternity from Bolton Priory, who 'perused with him the starry sky', or 'searched the earth with chemic fire'. But there were hidden forces in the Shepherd Lord only waiting the required moment to leap out in invincible strength, and the call came when the men from Craven sprang to the aid of Stanley's 'lovely wights' to fight at Flodden Field as seldom men had fought before. A great ballad of the age, throbbing with life and ablaze with enthusiasm, tells of the marvels wrought that day, of the terrors of the onslaught, of the rain of arrows, of the toe-to-toe encounters, of the retreats and the rallyings, and of the unceasing valour of the Shepherd Lord in the midst of the battle until victory crowned his side. And when he returned in triumph to Barden it was with his monarch's greatest prize, three of the seven 'Sisters' —the matchless culverins which had wrought such havoc against King Jamie and the ten thousand warriors who lay prone on the ground. Then forthwith he forgot glory, and went to his studies, and for ten years more until his death was the Shepherd Lord again, the scholar, the thinker, perchance the magician. The broken towers of Barden are his monument, and Bolton is his resting-place where the wanderer

> Walks amid the mournful waste
> Of prostrate altars, shrines defaced,
> And floors encumbered with rich show
> Of fret-work imagery laid low ;
> Paces softly, or makes halt
> By fractured cell, or tomb, or vault,
> And sculptured forms of warriors brave . . .

CHAPTER V

IDYLLS OF THE DALES

AN itinerary of the 'Dales'—a little exploring of their 'loops and links', a glance here and there at towns and hamlets, occasional loiterings in places where history is stored, and long pauses to capture their wild beauty—the dales and their rivers whose names in unison have a musical lilt and cadence, Nidderdale, Wensleydale, Wharfedale, Swaledale; we will fare forth to discover the charm they weave and the spell they cast. Flash of streamlet and dusk of wood; bursts of greenery that swell and stretch to the horizon; gentle glades and rocky fells; sullen-purple moors and splashing falls; ruined shrines and

> Rocks and winding scars,
> Where deep and low the hamlets lie
> Beneath their little patch of sky
> And little lot of stars;

this is the changeful panorama. It has provided inspiration for poet and artist; many novelists have made it the environment of their romances, and dramatists have found it a fitting background for their plots. Gay or sombre, the dales and moors are full of suggestion for the dreamer—a Wordsworth plucks a legend, a Brontë plunges in tragedy. Whether such rapture and keenness be ours or not we shall understand somewhat of the glamour and witchery of the scenes. A path winds through Nidderdale, where the melodious ripple of the river is often the only break in the drowsy region. Sometimes it croons by meadow and delicate woodland; sometimes with faintest cadence runs smooth and glistening in the sunshine; now it slips through sheltered stretches beyond the light; and now it is gulped into dim caverns, presently to emerge with a sudden splash and pursue a rolling course over rocks and boulders till white with foam it sinks again into a placid pool.

The Nidd draws us to Knaresborough, with its houses pitched upon a side of the cliff the river bathes, and where from the high bridge may be seen the revels of summer festivals. A first glimpse sets the fancy astir, and the Norman castle standing on the rock revives memories of times of turbulence when De Montfort and De Burgh made bold bids for power, and when John of Gaunt raised the massive keep. Gloomy dungeons and secret passages might yield ghostly stories for Monk Lewis; legends are many, history supplies strange and moving themes. Hither à Becket's murderers fled from justice before making their way to the Holy Land. The castle witnessed some of the final events in the Civil War; stoutly held by the Cavaliers, it was besieged and taken by the Roundheads under Fairfax, and four years after Marston Moor it was left to ruin. A story of those days concerns a youth's effort to assist his father in the garrison, where men were starving. Every night the lad crossed the dry moat, climbed the precipitous walls, and pushed a little store of food through a gap into his father's hands. At length he was detected; the soldiers' fire brought him down, and he was marched before a tribunal. The sentence, to strike terror into others, was that he should be hanged in sight of the besieged men. Then comes the sparkle of

KNARESBOROUGH

romance. A lady interceded for his life, and the heart of the surly Lilburne was touched. He granted a respite, and when the castle capitulated and the troops departed father and son met again.

Designed by nature as a bulwark, Knaresborough was occupied by Roman and Saxon. But we know nothing of their deeds. The first chronicler was the inevitable Leland, who 'numbred 11 or 12 towres in the walles of the castel, and one very fayre beside in the second area'. In one of those prison towers dwelt a while the hapless Richard, eating out his heart, and in the mood to meditate here as at Pontefract that he had wasted time, that time had wasted him:

> And these external manners of laments
> Are merely shadows to the unseen grief,
> That swells with silence in the tortur'd soul.

Nature contrived with men to make the rocks and caves of Knaresborough places of awe. It has a Devil's Crag, weird caverns, and a dropping well with petrifying waters; a Lytton was needed with his art of description, his touch of exaggeration, and his love of the supernatural, to do justice to their rude and provocative aspect. Recalling the tradition of the saint who gave his name to the cave, he related that 'on the banks of the River Nidd, whose waters keep an everlasting murmur to the crags and trees that overhang them', was the hermitage of one of those enthusiasts 'who made their solitude in the sternest recesses of the earth, and from the austerest thoughts and the bitterest penance, wrought their joyless offerings to the great Spirit of the lovely world. This desolate spot was called from the name of its once-celebrated eremite, St. Robert's Cave.' Traversing a narrow path through the tall wet herbage along the brink of the stream, travellers heard an ever-increasing and deafening sound of the waters. 'And presently,' says the wonder-loving novelist, 'the glimmering and imperfect light of the skies revealed the dim slope of a gigantic rock that rose abruptly from the middle of the stream. Rude, barren, vast, as it really was, it seemed by the uncertainty of night like some monstrous and deformed creature of the waters suddenly emerging from their vexed and dreary depths. This was the far-famed Crag which had borrowed from tradition its evil and ominous name.' This stream, bending round 'with a broad and sudden swoop', and 'ghostly and indistinct through the darkness', led to the waterfall. 'Only in one streak adown the giant cataract the stars were reflected; and this long train of broken light glittered preternaturally forth through the rugged crags and sombre verdure that wrapped either side in utter and rayless gloom. Incessant and eternal the waters thundered down into the gulf; and then, shooting over that fearful basin and forming another but mimic fall, dashed on, till they were opposed by a sullen and abrupt crag below; and besieging its base with a renewed roar, sent their foamy and angry spray half way up the hoar ascent.'

Superfluous to say that these lurid passages are from *Eugene Aram*, that melodramatic semi-historical work based upon a tragedy of which Knaresborough would be rid if it could. No need for long detail of the crime for which the young usher and recluse was condemned. A man named Clarke had been murdered, and the guilt lay between Aram and a disreputable associate, Houseman. To save his neck, Houseman turned informer, and his uncorroborated word procured a verdict. Aram might have escaped but for his own

ST. ROBERT'S CAVE, KNARESBOROUGH

defence, which was too subtle and academic to move the hidebound men of law or pierce the intellect of a jury. A few plain, rebutting facts would have served better than a host of classical allusions. The rhetorical fustian of a confession which Lytton ascribes to Aram is, of course, a novelist's concoction, and poor at that; all that is true is that on the morning of execution a few lines were penned by the faltering hand of the man whose last hope was gone:

> Come, pleasing rest, eternal slumber fall,
> Seal mine, that once must seal the eyes of all;
> Calm and composed, my soul her journey takes,
> No guilt that troubles, and no heart that aches:
> Adieu, thou sun, all bright like her arise,
> Adieu, fair friends, and all that's good and wise.

Knaresborough inclines to credit Aram's innocence, despite the bones found in St. Robert's Cave; modern opinion agrees that the witness-in-chief bore the main share of guilt, and that Thomas Hood's lugubrious verses must not be implicitly trusted.

Pity that the spirit of Ursula Shipton, Knaresborough's witch, could not have been summoned up for oracular deliverance on a matter so occult. The derided prophetess, once devoutly trusted, was no myth, no bubble of earth, for a record is to be found of her baptism in 1488 by the Abbot of Beverley. And, to destroy any idea of pleasing romance, a contemporary account of her dilates upon her extreme ugliness: 'Her stature was much larger than common, her body crooked, her face frightful.' To compensate for these obvious defects her understanding was extraordinarily good That must have been her attraction for Toby Shipton of Skipton, a builder, who married Ursula Southeil and thereby immortalized his name;

and as a last tribute to her talents a monument was erected to ' one who never ly'd, Whose skill has oft been try'd ', on the high north road a mile from York. So Knaresborough has its history, grave and gay, and we may muse upon it as we make our way along the road that was constructed by ' Blind Jack ' Metcalfe, or peer up at the sky through the branches of the old oak at Cowthorpe, or glance at Hampsthwaite and recall that from a family there sprang the writer of *Vanity Fair*.

Proud as Nidderdale is of her beauty she makes no boast of her nominal capital, the grey little town with a steep high street and a church on a hill, Pateley Bridge. But it has a cluster of associations in which the names of Benson and Kipling shine out, for the ancestors of an archbishop are traced to the spot, and the father of a poet found there a temporary home as one of Wesley's missioners. The wild region where the Romans made their first road in Yorkshire to reach the lead-mines breaks into Rudyard Kipling's love-story of the soldier Learoyd, the parson Barraclough, and the girl Eliza Rountree ; and he called it *On Greenhow Hill*, from the remarkable hill which ' meets the sky ', as the people thereabout say ; a hill over which the monks of old led their pack-mules when the mines belonged to the abbot at Fountains ; a hill which many centuries before had known the settlements of British and Saxon workers. Men from Cornwall had come to the Greenhow mines and brought with them stories of goblins and fairies and ghostly creations of ' silver spirits ' ; they harkened to eldritch cries ; and phantoms rose from the bodies of those who had been entombed, killed by the slip of a ladder or the crash of a shaft.

A highway commanding views of the far-rolling

wolds and the vales within whose dimples lie the snug brown hamlets brings the traveller to a bleak and exposed tract upon which nature has wrought a fantastic phantasmagoria. Some convulsion in an undated past cast huge rocks into grotesque forms, many of them caricatures in colossal bulk of men and beasts and buildings. To these fanciful names have been given, and you move about among so-called temples, castles, and altars, and among animals which might be petrifications of prehistoric monsters. These are the contortions of millstone grit, standing a thousand feet above the sea, Brimham Rocks. They are scattered over many acres of ground, and suggest the startling thought of a dead city or the nightmare fancy that nature has been at war with herself and casting her massive missiles at random. As the rocks slowly perish at the bite of the blasts that blow so icily across the moors the forms subtly change as if nature were ever begetting things new and strange. Here we stand upon a giant's playground belonging to a bygone era which imagination conjures up, though to the geologist there is no impenetrable mystery. And quite near are the ancient sepultures on Graffa plain—the plain of graves.

Most of the old flax-mills to which the Nidd and her tributaries gave power in their working days are now silent, and even Knaresborough's once famous linen manufactory is a far-off memory. Near Lofthouse, amid scenes where the river fresh and youthful makes her winsome way, she takes into her rolling course How Stean Beck, a stream as lovely as herself and with banks beautifully decked. And here are great cavernous openings, Goyden Pot and Manchester Hole, into which the river plunges with shining courage, and after finding her way through the darkness triumphantly reappears. 'The Swallows' is the local name, for the dales-folk know the swift flight and dive of their summer birds, and how with their white breasts and flashing beaks they dip to the water and drink on the wing, and the sudden dive of the Nidd suggests a poetic comparison.

Robin Hood, who by prowess could pitch rocks from Whitby to Luddenden, might easily have cast one from Knaresborough on to the long strip of verdure at Harrogate, the Stray. The old Saxon Haywra-gate is the place of many springs, and since 1571, when Sir William Slingsby found their healing powers, it has been a fashionable spa. Its situation aids its popularity and the Bog Fields, Harlow Moor, and the Valley Gardens make irresistible appeal to the lovers of nature. The smell of the sulphur waters is described by old-fashioned writers like Smollett by an old-fashioned word which is forcefully expressive; ordinary wit exhausts itself in the epigram that the taste is nasty enough to do anyone good; science contents itself with the beneficent effect. Health-seekers and pleasure lovers are well acquainted with Harrogate of to-day; and a century ago it figured strangely in that most extravagant of fantasies, *John Buncle,* by the elusive Dr. Thomas Amory. 'In the year 1731,' he wrote, 'I arrived at Harrogate, in the West Riding of Yorkshire, in order to amuse my mind with the diversions and company of the place. It is a small straggling village on a heath, two miles from Knaresborough. The sulphur wells are three, on the north side of the town, about five hundred yards east of the bog. They rise out of a little dry hill. The second is a yard from the first, and the third is five yards and a half from the second. The water rises into stone basins, which are

HARROGATE SPA

each inclosed in a small neat building of stone and lime a yard square on the insides, and two yards high, covered over with thick flagstones, laid in a shelving direction . . .' And so on, with much particularity, the precise chemical details being highly scientific, and the medical almost Rabelaisian.

But the tribute to the healing springs is unalloyed. 'Whatever ails you, consumption excepted, fly to Harrogate, and the water will do you good, if your hour be not come: and if you are well, the waters will promote long life, and make you the more able to dance with the ladies.' At the same time the worthy doctor solemnly warned the patients to be extremely discreet in their meats and liquors. 'Be temperate and regular, use exercise, and keep the passions within bounds, and you may expect very astonishing cures, provided your bodies are not become irreparable, and no longer tenantable, your juices not to the last degree glutinous and acrimonious, and the corrosiveness of your blood not bringing on mortifications, nor inflammations, filling, dilating, and breaking your vessels into suppuration and putrefactions.' And having thus relieved his mind, and delivered a homily on 'Temperance, O Divine Temperance', he spoke of the company he found in Harrogate and of the manner in which the time was spent at the Spa in his day. 'In the daytime,' said he, 'we drank the waters, walked or rode about, and lived in separate parties; lodging in one or other of the three inns that are on the edge of the common; but at night, the company met at one of the public-houses, the inns having the benefit of the meeting in their turn, and supped together between eight and nine o'clock on the best substantial things, such as hot shoulders of mutton, rump steaks, hot pigeon pies, veal-cutlets, and the like. For this supper, ladies and gentlemen pay eight-pence each, and after sitting an hour, and drinking what wine, punch, and ale, every one chuses, all who please get up to country-dances, which generally last till one in the morning; those that dance, and those who do not, drinking as they will. The ladies pay nothing for what liquor is brought in, either at supper or after, and it costs the gentlemen five or six shillings a man. At one, the ladies withdraw, some to their homes in the neighbourhood, and some to their beds in the inns. The men who are temperate, do then likewise go to rest.'

It was at this resort that John Buncle made the acquaintance of those six Irish gentlemen in whom Lamb and Hazlitt found perpetual entertainment. They were, with one exception, handsome and rich; they were of genteel education and possessed of amazing faculties, and one of them was the 'profanest swearer I have ever known', a fighter, a profligate, a smoker who blew two pipes at once, one at each corner of his mouth, and threw the smoke of both out of his nostrils. Among other rare accomplishments, he 'drank seven in a hand, that is, seven glasses so placed between the fingers of his right hand, that in drinking, the liquor fell into the next glasses, and thereby he drank out of the first glass seven glasses at once, and he made but one gulp of whatever he drank; he did not swallow a fluid like other people, but if it was a quart, poured it in as from pitcher to pitcher.' This feat alone should have made it worth while to be at Harrogate in the eighteenth century, though concerning certain other of the gentleman's habits and qualities it is advisable to be more reticent than was John Buncle.

The lure of another siren voice is in our ears, and the Wharfe draws us to another dale and guides us through

HAREWOOD HOUSE

a domain of serene beauty. It has been a poet's pleasaunce. Thomas Gray chanted its praise, delighting in the prospect around Burley, which was to cradle one of his high calling, William Watson; and, long before, the region had nourished the youth of Edward Fairfax of Fewston who unlocked for English readers the charm of Tasso's *Jerusalem Delivered*. There is a monument to his soldier father, who discussed with Monk the terms of the Restoration, in the old church at Harewood, noted also for its tomb of the honoured Gascoigne of Gawthorpe, that fearless Chief Justice who coped with Prince Hal and his madcap companions. The castle in which John Baliol, the Scot, was feasted is a ruin, but Harewood House, dating back to the eighteenth century, stands picturesquely in the wooded park, a splendid edifice of Corinthian style. Its picture-gallery and its library are famed, but to-day the place derives a special interest from the fact that it became on her marriage the residence of the King's daughter.

Some miles farther lies Ilkley, where Roman Severus had his troops. Then it bore the euphonious name of Olicana; a Roman votive altar, with an inscription once legible enough to be read by Camden, signified that it was dedicated to Verbeia. Goddess, or nymph, or Queen of the Wharfe, which was she? It only matters that the Romans loved the impetuous river and that the proud prefect of the day raised an altar to the genius that presided over the Wharfe in her course from the hills to the Ouse. Ilkley, with its massive gritstone Cow and Calf Rocks, its bounteous moors where light spends itself in such cool clearness, its Heber's Gill, and its mysterious cup-and-ring stones, has sights and sweetness to bring the jaded traveller to peace. Of the fame of the moors who has not heard, if it only be in the words of the old refrain beloved of trampers: 'On Ilkley Moor ba't 'at'?

And there is Giggleswick, a very centre of antiquity with an old market on arches, old cross, old grammar school where Paley was a pupil, and the old, old cave high among the scars—so old that neolithic man, it is surmised, made it his abode three thousand years before the Christian era. Here are the moors' mysteries and marvels. As for wild scenery we might betake ourselves to the exposed heights of Penistone, famed for its cloud-bursts; or to the summit of Otley Chevin to overlook the undulating expanse of the regions through which the Wharfe quickly flows; or to the glorious disorder of Wharncliffe Crags—'still o'er their pines the summer dews descend', a wonderland of many trees, where 'the dark massive billows of the oak, the more broken waves of the ash, and the foam-like lightness of the birch, give to this ocean an aspect of magnificence heightened by the bold ridge of rocks which crests the summit'. Taylor the Water Poet visited the Crags in 1609, and wrote an account of the mysterious square stone with its engraving and of his entertainment in the Dragon's Den. The whole region teems with romance, and processions of early peoples seem to steal back along the pathways.

But the heritage lies not alone in the outspread signs of the past but in those which have to be sought in dark places. Even early legends, such as those of Arthur, fade away at Dowkabottom Cave, the very name falling with a thud on the ears, and the relics of the Romans seem almost modern when set against those of bygone ages which knew the primeval races who dwelt hereabouts before the Wharfe had shaped the dale. We are in the region also of Bolton and Barden, with stories almost like fairy-tales; in Appletrewick, resting in the shadow of Simon's Seat, we muse on William Craven, the merchant prince, first Earl of Craven, whose son wedded the Queen of Bohemia; we pass enchanting little spots like Hawkswick, Linton, and Arncliff; and nearer the strong lofty hills come to Kettlewell, Buckden, and Starbotton, and the sheep-shearing centre of Kilnsey; and then silence falls on Whernside and Buckden Pike, and from the side of Cam Fell, in an old world untinged by the new, the Wharfe is seen issuing forth, down the old raiders' way through Langstrothdale.

When Michael Drayton wrote that the Don

> Makes the three Ridings in their stories
> Each severally to show their glories,

he intimated that to whichever dale we turn we shall be rewarded with beauty of its own. Wharfe, Nidd, Don, Swale, Ure, guide us to glimmering shrines and picturesque mansions. In the county of many rivers the Swale holds high place, and is itself high-spirited as seen when clouds scud across the sky and the birds rise uneasily up from the banks, and the sound of the dash and swirl seems to foretell storm. Following the river from the high source beneath Shunnor Fell to the broad rich valley in which it joins the Ure to form the Ouse, the traveller must sway his mood to many changes. There will be stopping-places also for memories. Kirby-Wiske, the pretty village just within the dale, was the birthplace of Roger Ascham, Lady Jane Grey's tutor; and at Topcliffe is the green mound which marks the spot of 'Maiden Bowere', the mansion of splendid but tragic fame of the ancient family of the Percys.

Under Catterick Bridge a mile from the town the Swale flows on in increasing beauty, and over the bridge goes the old Roman road which has crossed the Don at Doncaster, the Aire at Castleford, the Wharfe at Tadcaster, and is now on its way to cross the Tees and take its leave of Yorkshire. Near Catterick Bridge the Romans established their camp as, likely enough, they had made their road in the track of ancient Britons. During the Great War the 'camp' became a camp again just as at Scarborough the site occupied by the Naval Signal Station was the signalling point occupied by the old Romans.

For some miles yet the historic places on Swale's banks speak of war and military power; the unsurpassed position of Richmond Castle, already casting its shadows along the river, indicates the sense of strategical values possessed by its Norman builder. The river, the woods, and the grey abbey ruins ahead make an unforgettable picture for the saunterer along the road from Catterick Bridge to Easeby, and the Swale, now leaping along its stone-strewn course, borders the grounds of the Abbey of St. Agatha, where of old strolled the white-robed canons and members of the family of Scrope. To Richmond from Easeby the river gains in grandeur, and at the short path's end the proudly-poised castle comes full upon the view, with the river half-encircling its mighty base. We leave the town with its handsome churches and its tower of Grey Friars sinking between the surrounding hills, and by Whitcliffe Scar, a wall of limestone rock fringed with the greenery of woodland, take our way toward the river's higher reaches, and pass Willance's Leap, where the runaway horse shot with its rider over the wall to take the terrific fall below. Richmond fades from sight like the closing of a great volume, or,

HEAD OF WENSLEYDALE

rather, like the pale, momentary luminance of a picture about to dissolve. Ahead spreads a wide expanse with scarcely a house to be seen—a background of nature without a human figure against it.

Out of the quiet of this landscape, across the bridge spanning the Swale, comes into view the village of Marske, with the tree-embowered Hall, the home of the Hutton family, from whom sprang in the sixteenth century Matthew, Archbishop of York, and in the eighteenth century Matthew, Archbishop of Canterbury. The lonely tower which stands on the banks of the river at Ellerton, sole reminder of all the efforts and prayers put forth by a body of Cistercian nuns, is passed; Marrick Abbey, the remains of a house of Benedictine nuns of the time of King Stephen, is reached; and at Grinton, with its square-towered church and its old stone bridge, we find ourselves in a village that wears with grace the honours of antiquity. It is the mother parish of Upper Swaledale and so far-reaching on its western side that it touches the Westmorland border. By Grinton Church, Swaledale gives away a part of herself to become known as Arkengarthdale from the stream that wanders through the strips of pasture-land below the hills that sweep down.

Rising on a vivid green knoll, as if proclaiming itself capital of Upper Swaledale, is Reeth, where the hills close in upon three sides of the little town and cloud-shadows rest on the great scarred moors beyond. On the wild waste of Fremington Hagg once strode a Roman pedlar, his pack, as we know from its unearthing after centuries, complete with those odds and ends with which every Autolycus beguiles custom. Little wonder that men who ventured over these lofty, lonely heights, whether Briton or Roman, should sometimes return no more.

And now we peer toward the hills which look darkly toward Muker and Keld. Given courage, you may climb to the high and houseless heath where the Swale has her source; but unless a neighbouring county calls, it is better to gain the wild and unfrequented pass to Hawes, the Buttertubs road, a name given to the circular chasms in the limestone rock like dark pits. Still mounting ledge by ledge, we at last see spread out, wild and desolate, a long roll of hill-country with Ingleborough and Whernside and Pen-y-gant seeming to ride in the heavens. Over the solitudes the eye wanders and scarcely detects a living thing. Above, a skein of wild geese are flying homeward, the last one honking as it goes, as if fearful of being left alone on the desolate height.

Wensleydale takes its name not from the river but from the town of Wensley; and those who dislike modern designations call it Yoredale, from the old name of the Ure. Into the Ouse, the central stream into which all Yorkshire rivers flow, the Ure falls with the Swale at Myton, and there we are near Aldborough, or old Isurium, a summer city of the Romans which the Danes 'dinged down', though legend attributes its fall to even darker powers. The same fate threatened Ripon, but it remains in its glory of to-day, the Minster standing high and looking down on Ure and Skell. Skelldale itself was in evil repute until a small group of monks settled under the beech trees, and the Cistercian Abbey of Fountains arose. Great names are evoked, the Nortons and Scropes foremost, while in Tanfield's ancient church the Marmions lie in costly tombs.

The scenery of the Ure grows more and more romantic as we approach the ruins of Jervaulx Abbey, 'once one of the noblest in England'. At Coverdale we are

GORDALE

in touch with Miles Coverdale who went from this secluded region to make his name as reformer and translator of the Bible. The Cover is a wild little mountain stream; the abbey is a hopeless ruin; but a never-fading field of quiet beauty remains. You see white cattle grazing in the pastures, and they serve to remind us that the monks bred white horses and exercised them on the training-ground at Middleham. At York in 1556 Sheriff Metcalfe met the judges attended by three hundred men, each man mounted on a white horse. And was it not a horse from Yorkshire stables that carried Charles II into London after the Restoration? Middleham Castle, with its Norman keep, dominates the moors. It is the castle which Anne Neville, the King-maker's daughter, gave with her hand to Richard, Duke of Gloucester, and until it tumbles to dust you will remember the ill-starred King, his victims, and the final tragedy on Bosworth Field.

Leyburn Shawl with its soft-sounding and comfortable name leads us out from Leyburn town along a terrace of limestone with woods and cottages, castles and churches, below, the grandeur of hills around, and the tremendous glory of the sky above. We look at the flower-strewn slopes and think of another of the chapters in the story of hapless Mary Queen of Scots.

The far horizon, edged as if with dark amber, makes a softly-tinted canopy for Wensley town. In the high churchyard, with the Ure rolling by, rests Thomas Maude, the Wensleydale poet, and within the church are memorials of many warriors of old, and the brass of Sir Simon de Wensley. The church imparts almost a cathedral air to the capital of the dale, and its history trails back to the days of the third Henry.

The river puts on speed, the scenery becomes wilder, and from under the bridge at Aysgarth, with its high-pitched sides, the water rushes along to the sound of its own hoarseness. Near the church the witchery of the landscape displays itself as in a pattern of brocade. The Force is the glory of the place, the river in spate, and with a deafening roar bounding over the wide limestone ledges which form a series of stairways carpeted with white dancing foam and walled on either hand by growth of living green. But when the spirit of the river subsides with its waters the dancing foam disappears, and only a few trickling rills, drops like Naiads' tears, fall from step to step, slowly to steal away and be lost at the clustering feet of tall reed-mace and wild iris.

There is nothing quite comparable with these cascades. Hardraw Scaur, formed by a stream but three feet wide as it flows downhill, gathering volume, leaps at last over ninety-five feet of cliff, clearing the face of the rock as it crashes into a pool below. Too fleecy does the foaming column seem, and too brightly shot through with silvery flashes, to cause the bellow of sound that echoes down the valley as we follow where the stream rolls on, sentinelled by tall dark firs, Akin to it is Gordale Force plunging over the ledges, and while we climb the steep buttresses the spray rising like steam stings sharply, and the waters bound onward with an exultant shout. To complete the grandeur of the scene there is massive Gordale Scar which rises in precipitous majesty in this amphitheatre of wonders. Then, amid the arresting views of quaint Askrigg, sliced as out of a grey old world, and once besung by Drunken Barnaby, there are the two waterfalls, Mill Gill Force and Whitfield Force, seething and flashing scarce half a mile apart.

If there are many tumbling waters, there are, by way of contrast a few placid lakes. One, reached by way of Bainbridge in Upper Wensleydale, where the Romans had their ramparts, is Semmerwater, of which there is a legend of a stranger, a poor man, who climbed the hills on which a proud rich city stood, and was rudely received within the gates, save in the cottage of a man almost as destitute as himself. In the rosy dawn of the day that followed the stranger stood upon a rock and pronounced judgment on the town that had despised and rejected him. Towers and temples tottered and fell, palaces and prisons, castles and cottages, all sank at the sign of the stranger's wrath—all save the cottage which had befriended him. Perhaps it is well that the blast of the horn from Bainbridge has been sounded for many centuries when evening falls to call all travellers down to safety.

Wensleydale ceases for us where the streams from the higher north—known once as 'Streams of Hell' because of the savage solitudes through which they come—join the Ure. The dale ends greatly, and as we look upward we see the mountain-points in the long range that seem to beckon to vast solitudes, unfrequented, almost unknown.

The itinerary ends, yet the half has not been told.

CHAPTER VI

THE HAUNTED HOUSE AT HAWORTH

UPHILL from Hebden Bridge you reach as wild and bleak a stretch of the Pennines as Yorkshire can show. The wind cuts keenly, but brings with it the sharp tonic savour of the tufted land ; it rends the low-drooping rain-clouds casting their deep shadows below ; it whines a melancholy melody in the ears. Otherwise all is still as we pass the ghostly guide-stoups that stand at short distances, like sentinels turned to stone, along the high winding road. Here and there a dark house with slated roof looms out forlornly ; now there is a crowded little cluster bearing a hamlet's name, with a sturdy church as a centre ; and so we come to Haworth, at once a surprise, a disappointment, and an exhilaration.

The narrow street pushing upwards and hemmed with dwarfish houses and mean shops is unlovely ; the church on the hill is too ostentatiously modern to satisfy mind or vision ; the old parsonage fronting a patch of bright garden has no outward aspect to please ; the environment is dull. An overcrowded churchyard with heavy blocks of gravestones completes the scene. Yet what could be more fitting if we are to understand the associations, and into a sombre drama fashion the figures of three isolated women whose spirits haunt the dreary place, who dwelt amid tragedies, who drudged and despaired and endured disappointments, who died young, but whose genius forced them into fame which defies forgetfulness and death ? It is the

Brontë land, where a harsh and gloomy recluse was fated to see his family wither, and was left in old age to brood upon loss on loss until he must have deemed himself in an abode of doom. If three daughters brought lustre to his name, a son sullied it with shame. In the church lies the dust of two who were his pride, and on the walls is a tablet crowded with the names of all whom he mourned. Sadder life there scarce could be than that of the Rev. Patrick Brontë, father of Charlotte, Emily, and Anne. Haworth is consecrated ground, a pilgrim's shrine, where we mingle thanksgiving with lamentation.

Beyond, far as sight can pierce, are the moors, almost eerie in their vast phantasmal sweep until they mingle with the misty pearl or grey of the horizon. A few grim rocks prone on the turf, a farm shut off from the world, an old house half-hiding its huddled form in a dusky wood, alone break the monotony of the landscape. In a rift may be found a chill waterfall. A once-sturdy structure known as Old Withens is falling into ruin. There are creaking doorways and gaping windows in vacant huts. A few villages timidly lurk round corners of the hills. There is a pervading sense of silence and loneliness around. And we are haunted by unseen presences. Surely at yonder gate stood inhuman Heathcliffe, and in that dismal wail of the wind we catch the sobbing cry of Cathy's ghost. The drama of *Wuthering Heights* unfolds itself behind this curtain of mystery and awe.

There are times when the moors beyond Keighley display a glory of colour as the heather clothes them with flushing purple blooms; but that is not the Brontë moorland. You must see the region dim or darkened, and, most appropriate of all, in sullen storm when the clouds are rent by fierce winds, when the long weedy grass droops under the drench of rain, and when there are voices in the air. Then comes understanding of the mood of the Brontë sisters who roamed this land, dreaded it, peopled it with wildness, and yet ever yearned for it. This abode of fear and gloom was their source of inspiration—inexplicable, for we are dealing with inscrutable natures, the only clear fact about whom is that they comprehended themselves.

The birthplace of the Brontës was the drab little town of Thornton, the old church now a heap of ruins; and the Rev. Patrick's coming to Haworth was heralded by tumult. The trustees objected to his nomination, and he gave way to the Rev. Mr. Redhead. Then the parishioners objected, shuffled their clogs during the reading of the Lessons, and marched out of church when the sermon began. One Sunday a man, wearing a number of battered old hats, rode up and down the aisles on an ass. On the third Sunday a drunken chimney-sweep led a rabble into the pews and interrupted the service. Mr. Redhead, threatened with violence, resigned; Mr. Brontë was accepted in his place, a well-meaning though querulous preacher, performing his duties with precision for forty years, living to be eighty-five, ending in blindness.

Charlotte, the eldest daughter, was only five when the perpetual curate of Thornton removed to Haworth. In the parsonage her two sisters were born; in the parsonage her mother died. For six years she was the housekeeper. At one period she took up her unfinished education at Roe Head, near Huddersfield, and afterwards returned as a teacher; it was there she met her closest friends, Ellen Nussey and Mary Taylor, the latter to become 'Rose Yorke' in *Shirley*. Of her

HAWORTH CHURCH

further education abroad, and her hapless love for the professor who tutored her in French, there is no need to speak here ; the three sisters were reunited at Haworth, and from the parsonage went the first volume of Currer, Ellis, and Acton Bell to be printed—and exactly two copies sold. The adventures with the novels, their many rejections, their ultimate acceptance, and the sudden blaze of fame, make a familiar story, but one that will never fail in interest. All these medley odds and ends fit somehow into a fantastic scheme, never complete, never quite comprehensible, until too late. 'What a story,' wrote Thackeray, 'is that of the family of poets in their solitude yonder on the gloomy northern moors!' and the tragedy is in three short sentences that stab like a blade : Anne, dead at twenty-seven ; Emily, dead at twenty-nine ; Charlotte, dead at thirty-eight.

Cheerless enough had been their lives. The inexorable father disciplined them well. They did housework, knitted, sewed, and cooked. Their relaxation was a walk across the moors with their dog. They did not freely converse ; they brooded, they imagined, and in time they drew from the recesses of their hearts their store of experiences, re-created to body forth their dramas. They were shy, reticent, aloof, and yet were forced to witness depravity and horror in all unabashed nakedness at their own doors. A tawdry, pretentious, shiftless brother, with a touch of artistic genius and with pot-house habits, kept the whole family in the shadow of shame, and stories of half-mad Branwell the boaster, seeking relief from a hated home in the tavern parlour, are still told half in pity and jest.

Charlotte's footsteps are traced to the school at Roe Head, near Heckmondwike, and to Spen Valley ; she found her curate Donne, in *Shirley*, in the Rev. Joseph

Brett of Oxenhope who wore out his shoes in tramping the country for subscriptions for his church ; and she had a love-adventure with the Rev. David Price, the young Irishman, curate of Christ Church between Laneshaw Bridge and Colne. There, in the prettily wooded churchyard, may be found the long Latin inscription to the lively and witty man at whose jests the sad and sedate girl was forced to laugh, but whom she could not be induced to love. His wooing was swift. He sent his declaration a few days after his first sight of Charlotte at Haworth, and he was rejected. Tragedy followed in the wake, and although he did not die of love, he passed away with suddenness six months later.

The sisters, as convention prescribed, taught in the dull-looking Sunday school which fronts the graveyard ; their own reading was the Bible, Bunyan, Shakespeare, Scott, Addison, and some formal eighteenth-century poets and preachers. Religiously brought up, they were heretics at heart. There were mocking demons within their outwardly placid form. The shy women thrilled with spiritual excitements. The lonely house and its fierce ruler made them the more furtive and secret. They scarce dare whisper to each other of their daring hopes. They were schooled to patience, though not to passivity, and they performed their tedious household duties with complacent ease. Yet they were seething with revolt. Beneath the subterranean depths all was turbulence and desperation. Charlotte was ardent, Emily impetuous, Branwell baleful—only Anne remained as calm as she looked. The spectres of insanity and disease hovered near. It was a home of foreboding and terror, a house of doom. Nor was the school at Cowan Bridge much better, for it added mental torture to physical affliction.

One brief spell of happiness was Charlotte to know in that menacing abode, a few months of wedded life with the David Sweeting of her romance, in real life the Rev. A. B. Nicholls, a good man with a very imperfect perception of his wife's genius. But so content was she that when the call came, ' Oh, I am not going to die, am I ? ' burst from her in agony. ' He will not separate us ; we have been so happy.' But the end could not be averted, and with one final gleam of light the darkness closed in upon Charlotte Brontë once more. ' I remember the trembling little frame, the little hand, the great honest eyes,' wrote Thackeray. ' A quiet and holy reverence of right and truth seemed to be with her always.' Though reluctant, she was not ill-content to die, for she had fulfilled her mission though she had not finished her labours, and her last message was resigned but still half-defiant :

> Well, thou hast fought for many a year,
> Hast fought thy whole life through,
> Hast humbled Falsehood, trampled Fear ;
> What is there left to do ?

Yet Charlotte's history, like that of each of her gifted sisters, is surely one of frustration, of promise and waste, of the bruising of gentle natures and of untimely loss. Emily died fighting : ' No coward soul is mine, no trembler in the world's storm-troubled sphere ' ; but Anne, schooled to patience, accepted her fate calmly, and almost deemed it well, only with a sigh of regret recalling the once-cherished hope :

> I thought that with the brave and strong
> My portioned task might lie,
> To toil amid the busy throng
> With purpose pure and high.

Charlotte's frame of mind when catastrophe followed on catastrophe, for she dearly loved both Emily and Anne, is exhibited in a letter of poignant experience: 'Solitude, Remembrance, and Longing are almost my sole companions all day through. If there were no hope beyond this world, no eternity, no life to come, Emily's fate, and that which threatens Anne, would be heartbreaking. I cannot forget Emily's death-day. She was torn, conscious, panting reluctant though resolute, out of a happy life.'

There was not so much a fretful as a resentful strain in the two sisters to whom happiness was denied. Outwardly they were placid, but the rebellion pent in their hearts poured forth in fierce torrent into their works. They found in the wildness that engirt them the very scenes for their moods, and the passion of the moors entered throbbingly into their stories of life as they had found it. The device of fiction does not conceal autobiography. The insurgent tones of Charlotte and Emily are heard, mingled with the softer voice of Anne, whose *Agnes Grey*, though it utters a protest, never rails. Of the three Emily was most defiant—defiant of fate, defiant of the forces that strove to subjugate her, defiant even of death always ready to strike. With all their rebellion, so just and so piteous, they are appealing characters, commanding sympathy, and dwelling amid benedictions. The moorlands are their mausoleum.

Yet at Haworth they were much like exiles, for they were alien to a race with narrow minds and repressed emotions. It was the land and not the people with whom their souls were in harmony. Here they found the material they needed, the wild scenes, the rough characters, the suggested horrors. Charlotte, who was never lavish in colour, caught a joyous thrill in describing the clouds moving down from the mountains : 'The hills seemed rolled in a sullen mist, and when the rain fell in whitening sheets they were blotted from the prospect, they were washed from the world.' Or take a Haworth scene of the 'boundless waste of deep heather, nothing seen but wild sheep, nothing heard but the cries of wild birds' ; or take the retrospect of the moors as a departing lover viewed them under a blue sky and with the sweet scent of the heath in the air : 'We reached the first stragglers of a battalion of rocks guarding a sort of pass beyond which the beck rushed down a waterfall', and where still, a little farther on, the mountain shook off turf and flower, and had only heath for raiment and crag for gem : where it guarded the forlorn hope of solitude and a way representative of the tone and spirit, of the sorrow, turbulence, gloom, and awe—with just a few fitful gleams—to be found in *Jane Eyre*, *Shirley*, and *Wuthering Heights*. Especially the last—the scenes must have created that masterpiece, the figures must have emerged out of that heavy atmosphere, the story must have been suggested by the loneliness and pathos of the bleak moors over which the wind sobs and the clouds lour. We almost expect to meet Heathcliffe ; we almost hear the wailing cry of Cathy.

Children of the moors, these Brontë sisters were mothers of moorland children in turn, gave them moorland names, imparted to them moorland character, moulded them in moorland form. Incorporeal though they be, they have the life, vigour, roughness, wildness, remoteness of wild hills and desolate places and broken powers ; the rage of the elements is theirs, the gust and the tempest, even the very demonism of unrestrained fury ; and thus we get the birth of monsters, whether branded Heathcliffe whom nothing could subdue, or goaded Rochester who could only be made docile by faithful love.

Haworth, then, becomes weirdly fascinating by its associations. The forlorn parsonage, now the Museum, serves as a plain casket for memorial gems. It is still the Brontë home: time and death have not effaced their marks or eliminated their presence. The three sisters are there, inevitable ghosts, and we watch them in every stage of life from infancy to womanhood. The brooding, malignant brother is there, frittering away the hours, the insignificantly small man with ferrety eyes, red hair, weak features, and a swagger, ending his futile career in opium, and, for a brief half-hour of heroic effort, dying on his feet. Charlotte is there, planning, hoping, unceasingly industrious; Emily is there, stubborn, contemptuous, neither loving nor beloved, holding riches in light esteem, careless of pleasing, demanding liberty, and encircled by dreams. Anne is there, quietly engaged on poem and romance, meek in spirit, gracious in act. And, in the end, alone with his sorrows, sits the sightless old father with his memories.

There is a pathetically intimate touch about the rooms; they bring us very close to those who were once their inmates, who flitted about the passages, sat at old-fashioned tables in the secluded quarters, fingered the cottage-piano with its tinkling notes, stitched their samplers, sewed their embroidery, scribbled in their school-books, even pencilled the whitewashed walls. These girls did not outgrow their childish toys and trinkets, and the father treasured their first handiwork, making careful note of their drawings and their early writings. We are impressed with the immense industry of the household : they found outlets for their energy in domestic work as well as in intellectual pursuits. The usual accomplishments of the typical young ladies of the period were theirs, and more, for their sketches were of no hackneyed character and their embroideries showed no mean skill. Their early ambition was to be country governesses, and they dabbled in everything to fit them for that high calling. We breathe relief to know that their printed circular offering service drew forth no response.

Meanwhile they occupied themselves with continuous writing, always ready with pen and paper, and when they were not composing they were content to engage in copying. No time was wasted. Tiny booklets filled with pages of cramped hieroglyphics testify to their busy hours. For pastime there were strolls with the much-loved dog who served so often as model for the young artists. Branwell, who painted passably, as the pictures on the walls demonstrate, may have looked somewhat askance at his sisters' pencillings and water-colours ; but their originality could not be denied. The old desks are there, empty now ; but how we should have liked to peep inside them and get a glimpse of the secrets they once contained ! So much is here to remind us of what the Brontë women really were, in their homeliness as well as their brief spell of greatness —whether it be a doll, a cup, a paint-box, a scribbled copy-book, a broken comb, a blunt-edged pair of scissors, or ornate shawls and a wedding-dress—that within these walls their very shadows seem to linger, and we should scarcely be surprised if we saw Charlotte bending over the study table with the manuscript of *Jane Eyre*, or Emily in her corner penning with nervous fingers a poem from her tortured heart.

In fancy we watch them don their kirtles and track

their way across the moorlands to that ' perfect torrent racing over the rocks, white and beautiful ', which had an irresistitible lure for them, and beside which they loved to sit in pensive mood. Or they would be found at Bleke Dean Trestle Bridge, spanning the valley at the head of Hardcastle Crags, and at the height of seven hundred feet inhale the keen, exhilarating air ; or wander near Wycoller Hall, the Fearnden Manor of *Jane Eyre*, on the insalubrious site where ' even within a very short distance of the manor house you could see nothing of it, so thick and dark grew the timber of the gloomy woods about it '—fit abode for the hapless Rochester. And most of all, for there is a special witchery in it, they would come to ' lost Withens ', with the mistal and barn, and the narrow leaded windows in the thick walls, and people it with uncouth and untamed Heathcliffe and his affrighted cowering company. Should we stand on a louring day on this forsaken spot we can still feel something of the terror which stirs in the heavy air, and we are in unison with the perturbed soul who had none but premonitions of evil as she watched its abiding shadows.

It is when we move beyond Haworth Church that we see the country opening out, the moorlands spreading before us with an eerie and disordered grandeur, and we know we are in the real Brontë land. And now the whole domain becomes animated, though it be only with wraiths. We are in the dim background of sinuous hills where the three shy, elusive sisters came, and from which by their spells they evoked the impalpable actors for their weird stage. There were, it is true, human prototypes, but they passed through alchemic change and were transmuted into prodigies. They were, indeed, often themselves and their companions,

'WUTHERING HEIGHTS'

but so wrought upon by their imagination, invested with such qualities as came from the power of suggestion from the engloomed wilderness, that they seem to be creatures of another world of being.

Charlotte wrote of her sister's magic conception an explanation specially addressed to those unacquainted with the locality, and unfamiliar with the inhabitants, customs, and natural characteristics of the outlying hills and hamlets in the West Riding. For *Wuthering Heights* is essentially a product of the moors, ' knotty as a root of heath '. ' Her native hills were far more to her than a spectacle ; they were what she lived in, and by, as much as the wild birds, their tenants, or as the heather, their produce.' And all is summed up in that wonderful interpretative concluding passage that *Wuthering Heights* was ' hewn in a wild workshop, with simple tools, out of homely materials. The statuary found a granite block on a solitary moor ; gazing thereon, he saw how from the crag might be elicited a head, savage, swart, sinister ; a form moulded with at least one element of grandeur—power. He wrought with a rude chisel, and from no model but the vision of his meditations. With time and labour, the crag took human shape ; and there it stands colossal, dark, and frowning, half statue, half rock ; in the former sense, terrible and goblin-like ; in the latter, almost beautiful, for its colouring is of mellow grey, and moorland moss clothes it ; and heath, with its blooming bells and balmy fragrance, grows faithfully close to the giant's foot.'

Heathcliffe's dwelling, ' Wuthering Heights ', took its name from a significant provincial age, so the author explained, descriptive of the atmospheric tumult to which its station was exposed in rough weather. The power of the north wind blowing over the edge was to be guessed by the excessive slant of a few stunted firs and by a range of gaunt thorns 'all stretching their limbs one way as if craving alms of the sun'. Seldom is the harsh picture brightened; seldom does the frowning and oppressive landscape smile in sunlight. The house is gloomy, and pervaded by gloomy spirits; figures move about in mist and cold; angry voices mingle with the gusts.

Tragedy hovers over those lonely hills where the wind wails and the snow suffocates. Cruelty, anguish, terror, and inescapable doom make up the drama in which a demoniac fury lurks. Figures which do not seem human pace the darkened stage, and voices utter curses and imprecations at which we shudder. The sky is almost always cloudy, the trees are twisted, the flowers blanched, and 'a fungus spreads its bright orange among the heaps of brown foliage'; everywhere we are reminded of withered hopes, bruised hearts, marred lives. The awesomeness both fascinates and repels. There are scenes almost beyond endurance, scenes of pity, scenes of torment, scenes of stark horror; and the last one leaves us gazing upon the bare grave of the devil-ridden man whom the affrighted country-people believed still to walk the moors.

Emily Brontë expressed herself, and her work was forged out of her experiences, her griefs, her struggles, her desperate flutterings against the bars of her cage. She was never more alive than when suffering and fighting, never more articulate than when bursting the silence with what had long been secret, never braver than when pouring out her heart unreservedly:

Let me be false in others' eyes,
If faithful in my own.

The moorlands were incorporated in her poems and romances because they were a part of herself. So it requires no superstition to feel that the spirit of Emily Brontë broods over this desolate region. She was kin with it; it was a part of her being; she absorbed its characteristics; she reproduced its weird life in her dark romances. Just as Cathy was part of herself, so the moorland was the home of her drama, and her chosen abode. We detect her phantom presence in the bleak places, where the stream dashes coldly down, where the wind mutters, where the clouds gather, where the shadows linger. The old farm falling into ruin is itself a type—it is meet that Withens should be deserted and broken, tenanted no more; assuredly it should be abandoned to ghostly hauntings. And who can say whether it be imagination or a subtle truth that the haunting comes from that untamable yet baffled genius whose spirit was so great and so perturbed, and whose short and wild career of sad but brilliant achievement was mingled with the sorrow and the suffering that the storm-swept moors symbolize?

Like Catherine Earnshaw, who dreamed she was for a short space in heaven, Emily always longed to be back in the familiar wind-swept moorlands desperately dear to her: 'Heaven did not seem to be my home, and I broke my heart with weeping to come back to earth, and the angels were so angry that they flung me out into the middle of the heath on the top of Wuthering Heights, where I awoke sobbing for joy.' And it was a cry from the heart when Emily put the words in the lips of another who found golden crocuses on her pillow: 'These are always the earliest flowers at the Heights—they remind me of soft thaw winds and nearly-melted snow.' 'The snow has quite gone down here, darling,'

Linton says to her, and then in one vivid phrase depicts the scene: 'I only see two white spots on the whole range of moors; the sky is blue and the larks are singing, and the becks and brooks are brimful.'

We see the grey solitudes, we feel the wind coming straight from the moors, we hear the bells ringing and the 'full mellow flow of the beck soothing the ear'. 'It was a sweet solitude,' we are told, 'for the yet absent murmur of the summer foliage which drowned that music about the grange when the trees were in leaf. At Wuthering Heights it always sounded on quiet days following a great thaw or a season of steady rain'—a nicety of observation and a particularity of knowledge only possible to one who felt the scenes intensely near and dear.

At the end of the drama we are still very close to the details of the landscape. Catherine's grave is 'on a queer slope in the corner of the kirkyard where the wall is so low that heath and bilberry plants have climbed over it from the moor'; and the lingerer under a benign sky 'watched the moths fluttering among the heath and harebells, listened to the soft wind breathing through the grass, and wondered how anyone could ever imagine unquiet slumbers for the sleepers in that quiet earth'. We are left gazing upon the smoking ruins of Wuthering Heights, and it is upon that ghastly scene Heathcliffe fixes a savage look as he broods darkly on the memory of the sole creature he had loved.

Well might Swinburne speak of Emily's 'tragic use of landscape'; her love of the moors, he said, 'exhales as a fresh wild odour from a bleak shrewd soil, from every storm-swept page of *Wuthering Heights*. All the heart of the league-long billows of rolling and breathing and brightening heather is blown with the breath of it on our faces as we read ; and all the wind and all the sound and all the fragrance and gloom and glory of the high north moorland.' We can pierce to the secret of the nostalgia of the Brontës, who ever pined to be in the region where they found kinship of mood. When in Brussels, with its gaiety, Emily was homesick for the moors and the ' piteous gravestones ' of Haworth ; here was her soul akin to nature. And beyond these scenes was that further vision of the resting-place where her immortal spirit should find peace, the undisturbed peace for one who had chafed against adversity and blighted hopes, who had resented the defeat of her desires and the baulking of her ambition ; and the sunsets she loved to view with a morbid delight only reminded her that ' parting day, however bright ', was ' still parting day, heralding night and the trappings of decay ', and that dusk with its thickest stars called her homeward to solitude and her own thoughts of hereafter. She was behind prison bars ; and the year's end, with bare trees, blinding snows, and tumult of storm on the moorlands, symbolized to her the close of a life-period and the entry soon upon a new existence. But she was indomitable, and waged war to the last—war against the world, war against fate :

> No promised heaven, these wild desires
> Could all, or half, fulfil ;
> No threatened hell, with quenchless fires,
> Subdue this quenchless will !

And so we turn from the little slab in Haworth Church which bears the record of the dates when Charlotte and

Emily Brontë died—but we know they speak, though unheard; are here, though unseen; that they have outsoared the shadow of our night, have awakened from the dream of life, and are made one with nature.

CHAPTER VII

ALONG THE COAST

ON a rare June day of pulsing light and tranquil air, standing upon a cliff above a little bay which curves a golden arm about the warmly glistening waves, you may see a sparkling coast-line stretching away and melting into a pearly mist, while at your feet is a sleepy town straggling down a zigzag path from the greenery and purple heather of the moors. Perhaps the view includes a ruined abbey or a battered castle solemnly overlooking the scene of quietude where only the gulls and guillemots

> with short quaint cry
> Just break the sleeping stillness of the air,
> Or, skimming, almost touch the level main
> With wings far seen, and more intensely white
> Opposed to the blue space ;

perhaps the shore will presently be dotted with the figures of fishermen, descendants of the old-time whalers, ready with goble and net ; perhaps a pleasure-resort will rouse to life with sounds of joy.

But whatever the picture may be, there is a little difficulty now in reconciling it with those wild and angry scenes of the past when the Northmen descended with fire and sword, when from age to age violent battle raged, and when these fair harbours were crowded with ships of war and echoed to the boom of guns. Whitby, Scarborough, Bridlington, Hull, and even the tiny places between, can show their scars and mutilations, and tell their tales of fury and conflict. Yet nature can be even more unsparing than man, and this blissful Yorkshire coast, a summer idyll of azure and gold, has been darkened by tragedies which show how remorseless are the forces at work. Ravenspur, once great in history, is but a wraith of the past—a reality become shadow, a dim memory, a name. It was, but it is no more. And strange it seems that the little red town of Beverley, set at the southern edge of the wold over which pilgrims of old came chanting their way to the Minster, was once a lively seaport from which ships sailed out manned by bold adventurers.

Coast erosion has caused, and is still causing, towns and villages to dwindle or disappear. But of many records of loss, that of submerged Ravenspur is the most considerable. The port was the Praetorum of the Romans, and a site held of such high import by the Danes that when they had descended upon the Holderness peninsula they gave it a name from the figure on their standard. That name the Saxons converted to Ravenseret, or ravens' shelter; then it became Ravensburg and Ravensrod, and during several centuries of prosperity it blazed upon the map as Ravenspur, outrivalling the King's ports of Scarborough, Grimsby, and Hedon. It attained to wealth and greatness; many ships, including ships of war, were in its harbour; its streets were crowded with traffic. In the thirteenth century the lord of Holderness had his manor there, and in the days of the first Edward 'Ravenser' sent two representatives into Parliament. Three hundred pounds had the rich burgesses paid for

RUNSWICK

the privilege of a free borough, and proud might they be, for Hull had only spared one-third of that sum. Every year the populace from afar flocked to the fair ; on two days each week they journeyed to the market. Stately buildings and many churches arose ; the monks performed miracle plays at the inns. Families of influence were founded, among them the de la Poles, who became Earls of Suffolk. John Taverner built the largest merchant ship ever known, the *Grace Dieu*, and was rewarded by King Henry VI with a special exemption from staple duty.

Far exceeding even these events was one which marked the beginning of a change in the destiny of the nation. Banished Bolingbroke 'repealed himself', returned to his country with uplifted arms at Shakespeare's 'Ravenspurg', and challenged the monarch upon the throne. Only some threescore persons saw his landing, but he had so joyful a reception that soon there were lords and gentlemen in his train, and the fiery Percys

> promis'd aid to bring
> Against their oath unto their lawful King.

So, with 'this king of smiles, this Bolingbroke', back from Ravenspurg, King Richard was made to bow his knee. As Bolingbroke marched on in triumph he rebuked a monk, Matthew Danthorpe, for erecting a chapel to the Virgin without obtaining royal sanction ; but, once enthroned, he himself gave consent, and added as a gift 'all sea-wrecks and waifs, and other profits and advantages accruing upon the shore for two leagues around'. To Henry IV, Ravenspur was a memorable and significant place, the stepping-stone to his fortune and power; after his death a lighthouse served as a memorial to him.

Then, when all was prospering and seemed fair, the sea swept in, a large part of the shore was carried away, the buildings were beaten down, and the people fled in panic. There had been warnings of impending depredation, but the disaster came swiftly. A terrific storm in 1355 whelmed the burial-grounds; two years later high tides obliterated most of the place. Yet before the history of Ravenspur closed there was to be one more event of moment. When Edward IV succeeded the deposed Henry VI he encountered an insurrection of Yorkshire farmers, and fled to France from the great force the Earl of Warwick mustered against him. He returned with 'desired help from Burgundy', and at 'Ravenspurg haven' he arrived as his great predecessor had done. At first there was scant prospect of success, for 'there rose on him Holderness men, whose captain was Sir John Westerdale, a priest'; and it was not until these foes were placated that his course became clear and the decisive contest at Barnet was possible.

Meanwhile Ravensburg was sinking, not, as legend declares, because of Edward's curse upon all Holderness, for there were more potent and inexorable factors of destruction which could not be overcome. The actual date of submergence is not known, but Mr. Beckles Willson, who has written the whole story so completely in his *Lost England,* puts it about 1530. The historian Holinshed does not mention Ravenspur. And the only known relic of the proud port, says Mr. Willson, is a crown and crumbling cross of beautiful design, which once reared itself before the church, or in the High Street, to commemorate Henry of Lancaster's landing. Beneath the swirl of water lie the ruins themselves, and only a faint chime from the depths detected in magic moments bears a message from some unseen tower to tell where Ravenspur was of yore.

This story, dwelt upon because of its singular details, could be repeated in general terms of Hornsea, Aldborough, Hartburn, Frismarsh, and Withernsea, upon the same imperilled coast. To some of them the fate came slowly; there were subsidences, encroachments, attritions, cliffs crumbled, houses fell, land was wasted and washed away. Time and again the pathetic sight was witnessed of dislodged coffins and floating corpses. The churches were often the last to go; high and sturdily built, they resisted the oncoming tides; but the builder's art could not withstand nature's attacks in the end. Hard rocky barriers alone could keep back the insurgent tides.

One such buttress is found at Flamborough Head. That remarkable promontory projects some five miles seaward, and the cliffs of limestone rock are the haunts of multitudes of birds—the cormorant, razor-bill, puffin, gull, tern, and guillemot, that 'pilot' which when swarming indicates the approach of a ship. Great caverns, including Robin Lyth's Hole, with their lofty roofs, and resounding to the roar of waters, fascinate the wanderer and reward him with glorious sea-views as he traverses the labyrinth. And at Bempton and Speeton, where the cliffs reach a height of four hundred feet, crowded bird-colonies are to be found, some, unhappily, to be threatened with extinction on account of indiscriminate slaughter in the name of sport. Thanks to the Naturalists' Union an addition has been made to the Wild Birds' Protection Act which caused egg-collecting to cease in June, and shooting not to begin until September, and as bird sanctuaries have also been established the beneficent work of preservation proceeds.

The coast is dented with delicious little bays behind which lie grey and red clusters of fishers' huts in streets crookedly winding hillwards. Such are to be found at Robin Hood's Bay, Filey, Runswick, Staithes, Saltburn, and Redcar, the most northerly resort. In her tender story of *Sylvia's Lovers*, Mrs. Gaskell transports us to the typical old fishing port of Monkshaven, the clues to which are found in her reference to 'Staithes' (the stone break), and the occupation of the inhabitants in the whaling trade, so that we know we are in Whitby. Very charming as well as precise is the picture of the moorland region, and of the purple crags whose summits are crowned with greensward stealing down the sides of the scaur in grassy veins. 'In the moorland hollows, trees and underwood grew and flourished, so that, while on the bare swells of the high land you shivered at the waste desolation of the scenery, when you dropped into these wooded bottoms you were charmed with the nestling shelter which they gave.' A vivid depiction follows of the moors themselves, here and there bleak, with the red freestone cropping out above the scanty herbage; then a brown tract of peat or bog, then purple ling on the higher sandy soil where the heather spreads in wild luxuriance. Little black-faced sheep browse on the tufts of fine elastic grass. In the vales, far apart, are old stone halls and farm-houses, with narrow meadows dotted with stunted trees; and over the dreary region the sea-winds pipe, and 'great ghastly whale-jaws, bleached bare and white, were the arches over the gateposts to many a field or moorland stretch'. Not a pleasing scene, but fitting for a pathetic tale of press-gang days,

ST. HILDA'S ABBEY, WHITBY

when the men of the district were roughly seized for the Navy to fight the French. And, 'many a rustic went to a market or fair, and never came home to tell of his hiring; many a stout young farmer vanished from his place by the hearth of his father and was no more heard of by mother or lover.' All which is a slice out of the history of these little north-eastern towns and their fishermen. And Whitby, where Captain Cook served his apprenticeship on a vessel, has its full share of these stories of the sea and seamen.

Yet its history is really ecclesiastical. The Venerable Bede refers to this holy place on Lighthouse Bay; the Danes gave it the name of White Town, by which we know it; and in Domesday Book it is Prestebi. The abbey rose in fulfilment of the vow of Oswy, Saxon King of Northumberland, after his defeat of Penda, and the miracle-working Saint Hilda was the first abbess. The Danes ruined it, and William Percy the Norman restored it; at the Dissolution it was unroofed, and became 'a nest whence the night-owl may whimper to the brook, and a ribbed skeleton of consumed arches, looming above the bleak banks of mist from its cliff to the sea'.

There is no sharper etching than that graven in dark lines and jagged edges by Whitby Abbey lifting its gaunt and haggard ruins against the cold grey sky. The crooked outlines of the broken walls, the lofty arch which marks the framework of a noble window, and the slanting stone sides on the bleak height, have a macabrous symmetry still, skeleton remnants though they be. But the pathetic picture is softened, and its harshness subdued, when the vapours from below clothe it with a delicate mantle, or when the mellow evening light casts a tender hue upon the silent shrine in its mournful solitude. We summon up the spirit of Caedmon, into whose verse something of the wildness of the sea-swept shore seems to resound as he chants of the primeval time when

> Nor was here as yet save a hollow shadow
> Anything created ; but the wide abyss
> Deep and dim, outspread, all divided from the Lord,
> Idle and unuseful.

Whitby Abbey made a witching background in Scott's tale of *Marmion* for the retreat and refuge of Lady Clare and her maids ; and in entranced moments visions were vouchsafed to them of the abbess at her blessed labours :

> The very form of Hilda fair,
> Hovering upon the sunny air,
> And smiling on her votaries' prayer.

The lost bells of the abbey almost inevitably supply a legend. They were sold at the Dissolution and shipped for London. But the vessel would not bear them away. It floated out a short distance on a calm summer evening and suddenly and mysteriously sank. And at Hallowe'en,

> o'er flashing seas
> The echo of the buried bells comes floating on the breeze,

for the invisible ringers of Saint Hilda's are sending forth their ghostly music.

A curious annual custom was the *horngarth*, or stake

enclosure, mentioned in the abbey register of 1315. It had its origin in a dispute between an abbot and a de Percy, and was a penance imposed upon three persons holding abbey land who had killed a hermit while boar-hunting. The tenants of the lord of the manor who made the 'penny-stake hedge' were enjoined to drive into the shore on the south side of the Esk, at low-water mark, at nine o'clock in the morning on the day before Ascension Day, a certain number of stakes cut with a knife valued at one penny. Their labour was accompanied to the music of a horn. One of the grim jests was that this hard duty could be relaxed whenever it was high-water at nine o'clock on the day prescribed, the humour of which lay in the fact that Ascension Day is regulated by the change of the moon, and consequently the relief could never come.

As we wander about the shores where the Esk meets the sea we are reminded of the black shining stones of the ancient days when barbaric invaders

> Bartered beads for Whitby jet
> And tin for gay shell torques,

of the fashion which set in so vigorously in Queen Victoria's days, and of the once flourishing trade which has now become little more than a seaside pastime. For many centuries the digging and the carving of the mineral (if such it be) went on in this quarter, which nature seemed to have exceptionally favoured by strewing a valued commodity over a small stretch of coast. In the sepulchral mounds on the moors ornaments of jet have been found, and Roman and Briton alike had their bracelets of the 'Ammonite stone'. The love of our grandmothers for jet must have been inherited from a long past. It lay in profusion upon dresses of watered silk and bombazine, it sparkled on flounce and pannier, it decorated dolmans and tippets, it tricked out mittens, purses, and slippers, it bespangled mob-caps, and it composed ear-rings, lockets, and brooches. And Queen Victoria appeared in a bonnet with a crown of jet. The final triumph—for jet, now, is only, with cheap china and babies' spoons—'a present from Whitby'.

The coast swarms with bird life, and there was a superstition that the black petrifaction caused swooping flocks of wild geese to fall suddenly upon the ground, a phenomenon which in more prosaic times has been accounted for by the alighting of sea-gulls at Whitby in time of storm. The region where birds in multitude skim and chatter is Bridlington, the Burlington of former times, with a history dating back to King Stephen, who commanded the Sheriff of Yorkshire to allow the prior to hold it on the same terms as his ancestor had done; and what is now purely for pleasure was once given over to the coal trade with London. The event which gives Bridlington a page in the nation's history is the landing of Henrietta Maria on her return from Holland after conducting her daughter to the Prince of Orange. For those were times when the land was in turmoil and the royal family had aroused bitter antagonisms. Attended by a convoy of Dutch men-of-war under van Tromp, the Queen gained a landing despite the attempt of Admiral Batten to intercept her. Then the Roundheads bombarded her lodging and killed a sergeant; worse might have ensued, but van Tromp turned about and threatened reprisals, and another war with Holland was not in Cromwell's plan.

Scarborough, like Bridlington, is also linked with Stephen's reign. It was then a mere cluster of huts, but a castle was built on the cliff by the Norman, William le Gros, Earl of Albemarle and Holderness, and was destined to be the scene of some stirring events. Long before the castle-building Scarborough had known what it was to be invaded by the fierce Tosti, son of Earl Godwin, and his hordes; they had burnt, robbed, and slaughtered, as their custom was; and there is an awful legend that where the castle was afterwards reared these invaders piled masses of timber, set them ablaze, and hurled the beams 'in one great crimson drift of raging flame' upon the houses below, But after Harold and his Saxons had taken revenge at Stamford Bridge the Norsemen who had come over in five hundred ships found that twenty sufficed for the number who were left.

The castle of Le Gros was deemed to be impregnable and almost inaccessible to the enemy. Doubtless Piers Gaveston, the French craven and base favourite of the King, deemed himself secure when he was made governor; yet the indignant barons laid siege and made him capitulate to the Black Dog, Lancaster; and to his fate he went, with execration, at Blacklow Hill. Scarborough witnessed a strange scene on the occasion of Queen Mary's marriage to the hated Spaniard. A son of Lord Stafford joined Wyatt in his rebellion, and one market day he and thirty men dressed as carters, but armed, made their way with seeming innocence up the steep rocky hill to the castle, rushed the sentinels, and held out for three days. But it was a vain effort. Stafford went to the block, his associates were hanged, and 'a Scarborough warning' became a byword: 'A word and a blow, and the blow first.' The Roundheads had one of their conspicuous victories here against Cholmley, the Cavalier governor, seizing arms and ammunition, and capturing a hundred and twenty ships laden with wheat and timber. The castle gallantly held out, repulsed assaults, killed the General, Meldrum, and refused surrender for a year. But the fortress had been sorely battered, and how well the loyal garrison had endured is attested by the fact that when worn with sickness and starvation they were carried out in sheets to the streets below.

The history of the last two or three centuries, except for a startling episode in the Great War, has been of the social life of a fashionable spa. The virtues of the water were discovered some three centuries ago by Mrs. Anne Farrow, who, we are somewhat quaintly told, ' sometimes walked along the shore, and observing the stones over which the water passed to have received a russet colour, and finding it to have an acid taste different from the common springs, and to receive a purple tincture from galls, thought it probably might have a medical property '. With faith and courage the lady tried the water upon herself, found it had truly medicinal qualities, and noised its fame. But doctors disagreed, and though one of them declared its ' essence fit for the cup of a prince ', another offered a solemn warning against excess, illustrating his remarks by the example of a Mr. Westo who drank the waters ' not above two quarts at a time ' and found them so potent that he was ' put out of tune, could neither eat nor sleep, and not for a week was restored to health '.

Smollett knew this part of Yorkshire well, and chose Scarborough as a fitting place for Humphrey Clinker's adventure when he dragged his drowning master out of the water by the ear. But that resort of fashion was then, according to him, ' a wild common, bare and bleak,

SCARBOROUGH FROM CASTLE HILL

without tree or shrub, or the slightest signs of cultivation', and his Matthew Bramble lived there a frugal life, drank tea in the afternoon (on alternate days as the guest of the ladies, which was a custom of the time), and watched the dancers at the subscription ball. Yet there is a print of 1730 which shows a populous town, with ships on the sea, the shore alive with visitors, riders, bathers, and boatmen, and all the animation of a favoured watering-place.

To-day the picture charms, with the grey pile of castle ruin on the steep hill, shattered but with an air of defiance; while there is no more beautiful evening scene than that from the heights when the bay glows like silver, and the bold headlands, becoming more shadowy as night steals on, are steeped in a bluish moonlit mist.

Down the coast we go until we come to the King's Town upon the Hull, as the name went from the time of Edward Longshanks. Here the Lord Mayor is Admiral of the Humber and can fly his flag and be saluted with six guns. Here is the Land of Green Ginger, an intriguing mystery, the likeliest elucidation of which is that a green ginger garden was attached to the Duke of Suffolk's castle, and where there was a bowl alley still commemorated in the name of a Lane; but all are gone, and the modern post office replaces the ancient pleasaunce. Hull superseded Hedon as a port, engaged extensively in the whaling trade, sent men to search the polar seas, prospered, developed, and now proudly displays its seven miles of docks. When Cobbett visited it just a hundred years ago he called it 'little London', praised its cleanliness and order, and was delighted that it possessed 'no nasty, shabby, thief-looking sheds' and 'none of those off-scourings of pernicious and insolent luxury'. He objected only to the gilded equestrian statue of the 'Dutch Deliverer' who 'gave to England the national debt', and declared it ought to be replaced by one of Andrew Marvell.

And, indeed, to many of us Hull means chiefly Marvell, Milton's friend and coadjutor, parliamentary member, poet, satirist, wit, and honest man. He was not of Milton's inexorable temper, and his faithfulness was rather for ideal principle than for party creed. Good Puritan and ardent Republican as he was, he could still pay tribute to the merits of King Charles whom he opposed, and expose the weaknesses of Cromwell whom he loved. The Civil strife caused him grief, not bitterness, and he conceded to both sides nobility of purpose. But these things are of small account now except as casting light on the character of Milton's colleague in the Latin Secretaryship. There were two separate and distinct Marvells, the man of public place, and the man of the retired garden; the man who bent his mind to useful service, and the man who exercised his soul in flights of fancy. As member for Hull he was practical and conscientious, writing two hundred and thirty-six letters to the Corporation giving an account of himself and the affairs of State; as poet, he let his soul wander into dainty flower-lands where he could glimpse nymphs and elfin forms, gently philosophize with his coy mistress, or

> Through the hazels thick espy
> The hatching throstle's shining eye.

Could his spirit return, nothing would cause it more wonderment than to know that it is not as the politician but as the poet that he enjoys an ever-increasing fame —this genius who wrote only for his own diversion and relief, who published not one line in his lifetime, and who had been dead three years when a mysterious Mary Marvell informed the Ingenious Reader that she had found the ' exact Copies of my late dear Husband since his Death among his other Papers, Witness my Hand this 15th day of October, 1680 '. And it was in this manner that the world came to know the member for Hull as the author of the *Horatian Ode* with its political wisdom, *The Garden* with its delicious imageries, *Appleton House* with its magic flashes of description, and those lines on ' Where the rude Bermoothes ride ' which have found an abiding place in memory.

The lyrical singer has replaced the stern man of affairs. He did not realize that, admired as he was for integrity and zeal, he would scarcely have been acclaimed for three centuries but for the fact that by casting the body's vest aside

> My soul into the boughs does glide ;
> There like a bird it sits, and sings,
> Then whets, and combs its silver wings ;
> And, till prepar'd for longer flight,
> Waves in its plumes the various light.

Yes, Hull is the city of Andrew Marvell. He comes first, though we must not forget that in later time it could boast another humanitarian and patriot, William Wilberforce : to him be honour also.

CHAPTER VIII

ON HALLOWED GROUND

WANDERING on the Hambledon Hills, Wordsworth had his vision of the glories both of sky and earth:

> The western sky did recompense us well
> With Grecian temple, minaret, and bower,
> And, in one part, a minster with its tower
> Substantially express'd—a place for bell
> Or clock to toll from

—truly emblematic of that Yorkshire pageantry where cloud-forms and airy structures vie with the wonders of man's handiwork beneath. Temples, both of the living and the dead, catch the vision and enchain thought, the towers and pinnacles of cathedrals where worship has been unbroken for a thousand years and the desolated fabrics of sumptuous abbeys given up to silence and solitude. The array is amazing—York, Ripon, Beverley, Wakefield, Bradford, among the 'living witnesses' to the Faith; and Fountains, Jervaulx, Rievaulx, Bolton, Selby, Kirkstall, Roche, remnants of the power and grandeur of the past.

We take fleeting glimpses of many an ancient and beautiful sanctuary, lovingly hoarding its relics, in small and remote places: Driffield, the shrine of Saxon Alfred, King of Northumbria; Bedale, where a church in one of the most alluring of age-mellowed settings, shows its effigied monuments of six hundred years ago; Easeby with its Norman remains; Guisborough, whose history twines itself with the stirring adventures of Robert Bruce; Lastingham, with its unique crypt, a complete little church in itself with nave, aisles, and apse; Kirkdale, in the wooded glen famous for the Saxon sundial; Pocklington, where oak-carving is to be seen that Dürer himself may have wrought; Ampleforth, where the knight's head is pillowed on a woman's bosom; Tickhill, near the old royal castle granted by King Richard to Prince John; Pannal, fired by the Scots on their final departure; and Hedon, 'the King of Holderness' and Patrington 'the Queen'.

Elsewhere we are fain to linger. The square-towered church and the chapter-house at Howden on the Ouse still wear a majestic air despite both restoration and decay—a place of proud memories, where Bishop Skirlaw erected a palace, and where Roger, chaplain to Henry Plantagenet and the great historian of his times, had birth. In Camden's day Rotherham was famed for 'a noble church with lofty spire', as he recorded; and its pride was in an Archbishop of York of its own name, a man wise and prudent and beneficent, who established and endowed colleges and schools where boys were to be instructed 'in writing, grammar, and music, which are now suppressed by the wicked avarice of the last age'; he founded the church of red stone which served as 'a complete model of the ecclesiastical architecture of England in its purest period'. And there is Pickering, once in the midst of a royal forest, where fifteenth-century wall-paintings have been uncovered, one of them depicting Saint Catherine of Alexandria, the wife of the Governor of York who was the father of the great Constantine.

The Primate of England is Archbishop of York, and of the majestic edifice in the oldest city something already has been said—of its Saxon origin, of its history, of its superb architecture, of its accumulated treasures. The second oldest city in England, Ripon, retains so much of a medieval character that as we stand in its quiet streets we easily conjure up old-time scenes when true steel rowels were the labour of skilled and faithful hands, when woollens were manufactured, when crowds thronged to the horse-fairs, and when (as now) the horn was blown thrice at nine o'clock, and should a robbery take place the wakeman was responsible as not having taken proper precautions for the safety of citizens who had trusted him in return for their annual twopenny tax. A custom a thousand years old, piously preserved, and the Wakeman's House a substantial reminder of the fact.

Alfred the Great granted Ripon its corporation, and Eata of Melrose founded the Abbey. August processions still celebrate the return of Saint Wilfrid from the Holy Land, for Ripon ever dreams of the past. The Minster rose when Wilfrid became Bishop of Northumbria, and when he died miracles were worked at his tomb. Many years inevitably brought changes due both to devastation and reconstruction; the spires disappeared from the towers; Norman and Early English architecture intermingled. To-day admiration is commanded by the exquisite west front, the beautiful tracery of the east window, and the workmanship of the carved choir stalls; while the Saxon crypt with the narrow perforated niche—the 'needle to be threaded' by women who could prove their purity—remains for wonder.

We pass from the shrine of Saint Wilfrid at Ripon to the shrine of Saint John at Beverley, where rises the Minster which has been declared to be the most

THE EAST WINDOW, BEVERLEY MINSTER

beautiful Gothic building in our land. It dates to the eighth century, and so deep was the reverence for the saintly founder that even the ravaging Conqueror spared it for his sake. Saint John was a miracle worker, and yet it is not irreverent to say that his greatest miracle was the building of the Minster:

> this immense
> And glorious work of fine intelligence.

King Stephen bore his banner to Beverley for blessing, and victorious King Henry brought his wife Margaret thither to render thanks for Agincourt. Criminals had sanctuary when they reached the Saxon chair, the Fridthstool. The Minster was the resting-place of the great Earl of Northumberland, when, slain after a rebellion caused by Henry the Eighth's taxation, he was followed by ten thousand mourners, and the Poet Laureate, Skelton, composed his dirge:

> I wayle, I wepe, I sobbe, I sigh ful sore
> The dedely fate, the dolefulle destenny
> Of him that is gone, alas! without restore
> Of the blode royall, descending nobelly,
> Whose Lordship doutles was slayne lamentably.

The red-roofed town itself, with minster and with church, with memorials of early kings and the Percy shrine, with cobbled streets and ancient Bars, roots itself deep in history. In the golden days when the courts of princes swarmed with poets and minstrels, and when watchmen paraded the streets and chanted the hour and the state of the weather to music, a guild or fraternity of some consequence arose. These minstrels were wealthy enough to give a pillar to St. Mary's Church, sculptured with five coloured figures representing them in their costume and with their instruments, and the central character was none other than an alderman with robe and chain complete.

Arrestingly beautiful, Fountains Abbey was created out of storm. A bitter dispute led thirteen monks to secede from St. Mary's, York, and, without money or food, but full of faith and fervour, to betake themselves to a wilderness which eventually they were to convert into a garden. There is a tradition that these ascetic colonists of Skelldale lived under an elm, and during a period of famine nourished themselves on the leaves. Later they made a shelter under seven yews, some of which attained so great a girth that their canopy was serviceable as a roof. The monks laboured hard, and they slept on the ground. An abbey rose with glorious aisles and long corridors of stone. It was designed upon a great scale, as the noble proportions testify, and art and craft were lavished upon it to make it a temple of almost ethereal beauty. In time abundant riches flowed in, and the holy place became a treasury of jewels and gold. And the end was—the last of the abbots hanged and the fabric of centuries of loving care and toil given to decay.

Shattered as it is, roofless, and bare, it still reveals the wonder that it was in the glorious height and the matchless symmetry of its framework, and there is no fairer scene to be witnessed as we stand upon the undulating greenery which stretches afar to the dark borderland of the woods. It was a chapel of nine altars, vaulted cloisters rose three hundred feet, through windows of magnificent proportions streamed the light; and the grey walls were erected amid the spacious

ROBIN'S SPLASH, FOUNTAINS ABBEY

undulating green soft to the tread and reaching to far-off sombre woodlands. And now ?

> Sky-roof'd and bare and deep in dewy sod,
> Still 't is the house of God !
> Beauty by desolation unsubdued :
> And all the past is here,
> Thronging with thought this holy solitude.
>
> I see the taper-stars, the altars gay,
> And those who crouch and pray ;
> The white-robed crowd in close monastic stole,
> Who hither fled the world
> To find the world again within the soul . . .
>
> And, as our feverish years their orbit roll,
> This pure and cloister'd peace
> In its old healing virtues bathes the soul.

The Skell winds through the sylvan glade where the monks angled, and an ever-changing display of colour is backed by the dark hues of the pines. In a garden region near is Studley Royal, even in decay bearing witness to the charm of the past and to the piety and power of the men who reared a church in the old forest.

A band of Cistercians who had found no favourable ground in the northern dale came to the kinder meads under Witton Fell and built Jervaulx Abbey, and another group of the same Order raised Rievaulx Abbey in the vale of the Rye. Jervaulx shows a perfect altar with consecration crosses and some tombs of the abbots, but little now remains of the once sumptuous edifice. Rievaulx is a more impressive remnant. Direct your steps through an enticing wood, and presently you will find yourself upon the Terrace, half a mile of luxurious greensward where Greek-like temples have been reared; then the scene opens—there is a steep descent, and in the dale the broken outline of the abbey stands out, while far beyond rises an expanse of purple moor. You come nearer, and behold the Gothic nave, the transepts little injured by the despoiler, the roofless choir and the seven arches with finely wrought corbels, the semi-circular chapter-house, the choice Early English refectory—remains which make this early Cistercian house one of the most enchanting though one of the most pathetic of pictures. The romancer has seized upon it, and here Scott conjured up his Prior Aymer to play a part in the drama of Ivanhoe. As for the founder of this fane, Walter d'Espec, his eventful story is to be read in chapters fashioned in the glass at Helmsley Church.

Along the lanes and past the hill of the White Horse we come to another solitude where stand the ruins of the once-powerful Byland Abbey of Roger and the monks driven from Furness. Its three hundred years were of unusual placidity, and it fulfilled the idea of its founders as a place of meditation and repose. Until the final crash came it escaped the perils of the times and was happy in having no history. Under the careful hands of the restorer the jagged outlines are being softened, breaches healed, fallen columns replaced, and the whole proportions re-shaped. It will never be complete, but much of its pristine beauty will be revealed again. Byland was claustral in its origin, and the monks and lay brothers, in their different quarters, spent their lives together in amity, regardful of Abbot Philip's pious hope: 'And there, God willing, they shall prosperously remain for ever.'

On the banks of the Wharfe, before the battle of

BYLAND ABBEY

Marston Moor, halting space was found for the armies of Prince Rupert and Cromwell, and they bivouacked in one of the loveliest bits of England and looked down upon an Abbey even then venerable with age. An Abbey so-called, although it had never been one; the truer term would be memorial. The sanctuary at Bolton rose like a child of the river itself, born of faith, courage, and resignation.

> What is good for a bootless bene?
> With these dark words begins my tale;
> And their meaning is, 'Whence can comfort spring,
> When prayer is of no avail?'

Wordsworth told the old story twice in verse, the story of the Boy of Egremond who had been drawn by his leashed hound into the swirl of the Strid—

> Where the rock is rent in two
> And the river rushes through.

The bereaved mother, in place of fruitless grief, resolved upon a work of beneficence, and the Priory Church was her inspiration. For four hundred years the building and embellishing proceeded, and by carvings and window traceries the progress and change of the times can be marked.

> The stately Priory was rear'd,
> And Wharfe, as he moved along,
> To matins join'd a mournful voice,
> Nor fail'd at evensong.

Its history, after the Dissolution, merged into the romance of the Cliffords and the Shepherd Lord, whose tale is told elsewhere.

The lonely ruins are a picture of pathetic beauty, beloved of artists, of Turner, Landseer, and David Cox, the first making it a centre of dreams and enfolding peace, and so much did his soul command his brush that on his canvas he mingled its strength with its tenderness and its stern greys with soft reflections, and blent the pride of its towering rocks with the pebbles glistening in the river's bed. The vivid colourings along the valley, the fiery red of the mountain ash, the russet of the beeches, the yellow of the elms and sycamores, and the river, here broad and placid, crossed by its seven-and-fifty stepping-stones, are irresistible to the mind of the nature-lover ; and the sombre ruins of the old sanctuary add the final touch of enchantment to the scene.

The poets and artists of Bolton have also found at Kirkstall, 'where the dark pool reflects the chancel pillars, and the cattle lie in unhindered rest, the soft sunshine on their dappled bodies', a subject for pen and brush. A June sun lit up the ruins when last we turned into the grounds and caught the murmur of the Aire as it rolled down the small weir into the lower streams, our eyes drawn meantime to the royal colour of a bank of lupins standing upright as sentinels before the grey walls. In the footsteps of the pilgrims of old we could travel back to the mid-twelfth century when the Baron of Pontefract vowed to prove his thanks for recovery of health by rearing a holy place.

And of good Yorkshire stone the Abbey was wrought with the help of the monks from Fountains, and the stone is much in evidence—stone for the place of refreshment by day and for the place of rest at night, stone for the house of reception, stone for the hospital, and stone at last for the coffins, such as may still be

KIRKSTALL

seen, heavily hewn, with circles like haloes for the heads. The restorer is busy at Kirkstall, and we see him at his work as we make our way across the grounds, where the rounded fruit glows upon the cherry trees, and the music of the river, a silver glint through the sea-green leaves of the willows, is in our ears as we go through the old gateway into the open road.

A last visit transports us to Selby, with its legend of Benedict who had a vision of Saint Germanus and heard a message from his lips bidding him to build; and as proof that this must be truly done presented him with the middle finger of his right hand. Not much remains of the Abbey, though it once ranked for riches third in the kingdom; and, despite legend, it was held to have been founded by the Conqueror, and to have been specially favoured by him so that he granted the use of the mitre to the abbots, and to his glory and honour the choir were robed in red. Here in later days was Wolsey's summer house; now a few fragments give emphasis to the old lament of 'the futility of glorious structures which were the loving creation of centuries of devotion'.

Imagination peoples the soft green glades with the holy fraternity, with pilgrims from many quarters, with the concourse assembling for matins and vespers as the hush is broken by the note of a summoning bell. The scene of worship comes before us. The air, so silent now, vibrates with solemn harmonies. In sunrise splendour or in evening glow, and amid the sparkle of tapers, the statue and shrine are seen in their pure cold symmetry, and gleaming ornaments flash out a varied radiance. From the high windows 'richly dight' strike shafts of colour across the long aisles and break against the rigid pillars. The Church Triumphant for so many centuries—but the destroyer came, and behold ruin and defeat, the shattered walls, the crumbling stones, all that are left of the pomp and pride of the past.

What was, will be no more. The breeze sighs over the long grass covering the spacious aisles; in the crevices of massive buttresses flutter slanting weeds; their tendrils wind themselves about the framework of glorious windows. The high altars which blazed with light are gone, and the carvings on which men spent their loving craft are battered, obliterated, buried in moss or dust. At Coverham the very animals are sheltered where saints once prayed, only a few loose and fractured slabs denoting where once a temple stood. The holy places are for memories only. Where the air was flooded with chant and prayer and song no sound is heard but the hum of a laden bee or the twitter of a darting bird. The westering sun casts a mellow light upon the spectral stones, and the shadows fall deep upon the silent cloisters. Let us pace softly, for we are among the shrouded dead.

CHAPTER IX

TWO COUNTRY PARSONAGES

UNDER the Hambledon Hills, near Crayke Castle, and within easy distance of Byland Abbey, is the village of Coxwold, the most striking object in which is a church with a hexagonal tower. This peculiarity counts for very little beside the fact that this was the church in which the Rev. Laurence Sterne delivered his curiously original sermons, those ejaculatory discourses, half wisdom and half buffoonery, which must have bewildered if they did not actually startle a rustic congregation in the eighteenth century.

But Yorick needed a special audience, whether speaking or writing, and nothing demonstrates this more clearly than the words penned by Horace Walpole, sage of Strawberry Hill, concerning the greatest of his works. Nothing is talked of, nothing admired, said he, but ' what I cannot help calling a very insipid and tedious performance ; it is a kind of novel, called *The Life and Opinions of Tristram Shandy* ; the great humour of which consists in the whole narration always going backwards. I can conceive a man saying that it would be droll to write a book in that manner, but have no notion of his persevering in executing it. It makes one smile two or three times at the beginning, but in recompense makes one yawn for two hours. The characters are tolerably kept up, but the humour is for ever attempted and missed. The best thing in it is a Sermon, oddly coupled with a good deal of bawdry, and both the composition of a clergyman.' Walpole went on to declare that the great author's head, a little turned before, was now topsy-turvy with success and fame, and that his pecuniary gains had been considerable—six hundred and fifty pounds from his publisher for a second edition and for two more volumes ('which I suppose will reach backwards to his great-great-grandfather'); a stipend of one hundred and sixty pounds a year from Lord Fauconberg; and a purse of gold from Bishop Warburton, who paid him the compliment in contradictory terms that it was quite an original composition but was in the vein of Cervantes. After commenting on this, Walpole ironically adds that the Bishop recommended Sterne to the Bench of Bishops on the ground that he was the English Rabelais.

Can anything but anomaly be expected of this enigmatical country parson who preached twice every Sunday and occupied his mind with Uncle Toby and Corporal Trim on week-days, who divided his time very unequally between the pulpit and Crazy Castle, and who mingled scriptural admonitions with lewd narrations? Whether even yet he is seen in a perfectly clear light and is free from misconception may be doubted. There will probably always be controversy on his sentimentality, his treatment of his wife and mother, his whining over a dead donkey, and his lubricity in relating domestic episodes. None the less, the village in the region of the White Horse on the hill must remain a shrine for literary pilgrims, and year by year there will be unabated interest in the stone tablet over the entrance to Shandy Hall, which states: 'Here dwelt Laurence Sterne, for many years incumbent of Coxwold. Here he wrote *Tristram Shandy* and *The Sentimental Journey*. Died in London in 1768, aged 55 years.' The Hall, which was near the vicarage, but a private purchase, has been converted into cottages, but it retains its original picturesqueness, and Sterne's room, with its ingle-nook, has been preserved. Even the yew-tree beneath which he has been pictured as sitting in deep meditation—whether of story or sermon matters not—remains a part of the scene as Yorick knew it.

Sterne was no Yorkshireman, but in his autobiography he has explained how he came to be so long and closely connected with the county. 'I came to York,' he says, 'and my uncle got me the living of Sutton' (Sutton-in-the-Forest); 'and at York I became acquainted with your mother, and courted her for two years.' After describing his curious wedded life, he goes on to say that after twenty years of exile in the south he went back to York and published the first of his two Shandy volumes. 'In that year [1760] Lord Fauconberg presented me with the curacy of Coxwold: a sweet retirement.' Seven years later he left Yorkshire for London, taking with him *The Sentimental Journey*, which he had written the preceding summer at Coxwold. It was while he was settled in Yorkshire, so Sir Walter Scott in his biography tells us, that he devoted most of his time to books, fiddling, and painting. The books were supplied from Skelton Castle, where abode his friend and relation, John Hall Stevenson, a coarse jester, notorious for that wild and none too decent collection known as *Crazy Tales*, 'Crazy' being the name not unfittingly given to the castle itself. In the library Sterne found the antiquarian books from which he so cunningly plagiarized; and it was probably from Stevenson himself he acquired that peculiar vein of humour, absurdity, whimsicality, grotesqueness, and sentiment with which Yorick's name will ever be associated. And if Crazy Castle provided an atmosphere, one Yorkshire celebrity at least supplied a prototype, for Dr. Burton, a Jacobite whom Sterne hated, was Dr. Slop, with his quackery and obstetrical engines.

The parson who was to enjoy European celebrity for a unique style, and who had neither predecessor nor successor in the realm of literature, could scarcely have impressed the simple populace to whom he ministered at Coxwold, Sutton, and Stillington. Gray said that as you read Sterne's sermons you feel that he is 'tottering on the verge of laughter, ready to throw his periwig in the face of the congregation', and it cannot be imagined that this would have been welcomed by the people occupying those seats which Sterne himself had suggested should be arranged, some facing the pulpit and some opposite to it, 'so that those who approve of the vicar can face him, and those who don't can face the other way'. And actually this suggestion was adopted, and box-pews with seats all round were introduced, with the pew of the Newburgh family elevated and commanding a view over the whole of the church. Sterne does not appear to have been neglectful, but he was decidedly eccentric; we may venture on a little dubiety as to his earnestness and sincerity in at least some portions of his routine labours; and it is as a writer, *sui generis*, and not as a country incumbent, that his name is known after a century and a half. While we find twenty years of his life spent in 'the sweet retirement', his whole life of thought was elsewhere; and while in any circumstances or in any locality he might have produced most of his volumes, *Tristram Shandy* must be regarded as Yorkshire in its inspiration, its atmosphere, and its texture. It was conceived at Crazy Castle and created at Shandy Hall.

If we are sometimes inclined to blush for the parson of Coxwold, we have nothing but heart-warmth for the parson of Foston-le-Clay. For he was none other than Sydney Smith, preacher, writer, reformer, wit, and eminent as each. 'The greatest master of ridicule since Swift,' declared Scott; but he might justly have added of ridicule used for the noblest purpose. His career was almost a comedy, and lucky for him and for the world it was that his genius and his sense of humour broke down all obstacles to his progress and fame. He married young a lady whose dowry was six small silver tea-spoons; he projected the *Edinburgh Review* on a little oatmeal; he 'discharged' in London 'a few random sermons—the clerk as pale as death in helping me off with my gown for fear I should bite him'; he threw himself with ardour, and prematurely, into the work of political reform; he lectured on moral philosophy, 'of which I knew nothing, but I was thoroughly aware that I wanted two hundred pounds to furnish my house'; and in the end he was rewarded with the living of Foston-le-Clay, with a stipend of five hundred pounds, by his Whig friends.

But the church, one of the oldest in England, mentioned in Domesday Book of 1085, was only a barn; there was no parsonage, and for a hundred and fifty years no clergyman had resided there. So Sydney Smith obtained exemption, and spent his time during the next two years in writing the stinging Letters of *Peter Plymley to his brother Abraham* on Catholic Emancipation. But in so doing he grievously upset the new Perceval Ministry, and when the Clergy Residence Bill became law he was sent packing from London and crowded congregations to the obscure Yorkshire living. 'There was no house, no garden, only a bare field,' he told Macaulay. Under these conditions he started life afresh at the age of thirty-eight; and he started courageously. The wilderness was to become a garden; the man of intellectual force was to be the model country pastor tending his rural flock.

In those days Foston, between York and Malton, was off the main track, and the population was chiefly housed a mile off at Thornton. Sydney Smith hired a cottage at Heslingden, and for the next four years drove over every Sunday to his church. He turned himself into a farmer, an architect, and a builder; he cultivated his glebe, and he designed his new residence. Difficulties still beset him. The hundred and fifty thousand bricks he ordered proved to be worthless; the yoke of oxen would not draw them; his helpers failed him; a severe frost came and he had to go into the house when it was only half ready. On the way the family coach stuck in the road; his wife, carrying a three months' child, tramped across the fields and lost her shoes; and their first meal was a tea on the furniture boxes. Undaunted, Sydney Smith saw only the humourous side of this; happily, so did his wife. And before long the many-windowed, bright and airy parsonage, with its flanking lawns and clambering flowers, took shape among the sheltering trees, and, as Macaulay declared some years later after a visit, was 'the neatest, most commodious, and most appropriate rectory I ever saw'. Every night Sydney Smith, whose principle it was that abundance of light improved animal spirits, sat in a room 'illuminated like a town after a great naval victory'.

'I had little furniture,' he said, 'so I bought a

cartload of deals, took a carpenter (who came to me for parish relief) called Jack Robinson, with a face like a full moon, into my service; established him in a barn, and said—"Jack, furnish my house." You see the result!' This is not altogether a fantasy. Jack made the famous chair which Sydney Smith used in his study; and when he left Foston it passed as a gift into the hands of an old servant who was told to 'keep it in memory of me'. From 1809 to 1829, 'the best years of my life', Sydney Smith worked ungrudgingly for his little flock. He did not lose touch with his literary friends, and the home-built vestry welcomed at times such illustrious men of the day as Macaulay, Jeffrey, Brougham, and Macintosh. That Smith was happy is certain, for it was his nature to be so; that he was satisfied is doubtful, but he made no complaint of baulked ambition; that he was a good parson and a noble man requires no argument. Foston is the evidence. There was no petulance in his nature. To Lady Holland he had once said, and he meant it and proved it, 'If it be my lot to crawl, I will crawl contentedly; if to fly, I will fly with alacrity. But as long as I can avoid it I will never be unhappy.' Yet no man had been put to a more severe test than he in that neglected part of the world with its few cottages and 'a miserable little hovel with a wooden belfry' for a church.

During those years his ardour was unabated and his labours were continuous; his reputation for wit grew. Tom Moore in his *Journal* has recorded how irresistible he was. Poverty only seemed to increase his resourcefulness and stimulate his exertions. Whilst at Foston he needed a carriage, and his description of how he obtained one is too good to be lost. 'I discovered in the back settlements of a York coachmaker,' he says, 'an ancient green chariot, supposed to have been the earliest invention of the kind. I brought it home in triumph to my admiring family. Being somewhat dilapidated, the village tailor lined it, the village blacksmith repaired it; nay, but for Mrs. Sydney's earnest entreaties, we believe the village painter would have exercised his genius upon the exterior; it escaped this danger, however, and the result was wonderful. Each year added to its charms: it grew younger and younger; a new wheel, a new spring; I christened it the Immortal; it was known all over the neighbourhood; the village boys cheered it, and the village dogs barked at it.'

He was too thoroughgoing and too progressive to secure the accord of all his clerical brethren, and there were occasional meetings in Yorkshire at which he was not popular. However strongly he argued, he kept his temper, and he took his defeats with the customary good humour. Sometimes he had neat revenges in witty passages which, we are assured, gave no offence. He announced on one occasion that the human race could be separated into three classes—men, women, and clergymen; and on another he observed that people were ready enough to act the Good Samaritan 'without the oil and the twopence'. On the departure of the Bishop of New Zealand for his diocese, Sydney Smith recommended him to have regard to the minor as well as to the graver duties of his station—to be given to hospitality, and in order to meet the tastes of his native guests 'never to be without a smoked little boy in the bacon-rack, and a cold clergyman on the sideboard'. 'And as for yourself, my lord,' he concluded, 'all I can say is, that when your new parishioners *do* eat you, I sincerely hope you may disagree with them.'

The subject of Sydney Smith is full of temptations, and we must refrain. We have only to consider him here as a Yorkshire parson who, possessed of rare talents, and fired with high ambition, was ready when called upon to devote himself whole-heartedly to the humbler duties laid upon him. He visited the poor and afflicted, he preached wholesome sermons, he made himself beloved. He was 'village parson, village doctor, village comforter, and village magistrate'. Above all, he set an example of cheerfulness and courage more potent in its practical way than any outburst of eloquence or scintillation of wit would possibly have been. Wit itself is often caustic and hurts. Sydney Smith's was keen but kindly, and it is apposite to recall that when he was leaving London for Yorkshire Lord Dudley uttered these parting words: 'You have been laughing at me constantly, Sydney, for the last seven years, and yet in all that time you never said a single thing to me that I wished unsaid.' His name stands for good nature, and his life-work shines out as a gleam from the obscure little place where he gave ungrudging service. He hated humbug, had no pride, sought no preferment—though it came at last in the form of a canonry; 'For,' said he, 'when I was about twenty I made a most valuable discovery, and that was, that the rest of the world was not exclusively occupied in observing me.' But, as events proved, even Foston-le-Clay could not hide him, although the parish itself raised no memorial to him, nor, as a biographer wrote, inscribed a single line to show that he had ever entered its pulpit.

What matters it? We have his example, and we have from him that best of messages: 'Genuine and innocent wit is the flavour of the mind. Man could direct his ways by plain wisdom, and support his life by tasteless food ; but God has given us wit and flavour, and laughter and perfumes, to enliven the days of man's pilgrimage, and to " charm his pained steps over the burning marl ".'

CHAPTER X

TOWNS AND TRADITIONS

NO one could dispute the just position of York, by reason of antiquity and history, as the county capital; but Leeds and Sheffield hold preeminence as commercial centres. The Flemings helped to establish the great wool-industry in the sixteenth century, and the fame of the steel blade was celebrated even in Chaucer's time. Leeds (despite Kirkstall, her proud inheritance) may be regarded as typical of the trading city of material growth and civic expansion; but such places are not, as Matthew Arnold would have expressed it, steeped in sentiment, nor could that be expected; the spirit that animates them is practical, and the source of their inspiration must be sought rather in the Benthamite gospel of utility than in the ideals of Pericles. They are substantially alive, and with that are content. Huddersfield would smile at the claims of long descent, but proudly shows her cloth; Barnsley professes to no historic importance, but displays her excellent linen; Bradford is famed less for the chronicles of the manor of the de Lacys than for her worsted yarn; and Batley, termed the home of innocent imposture since Benjamin Law established a thriving trade in the rag-wool called 'shoddy', is probably quite satisfied with the soothing testimonial of an old writer that the 'business of adulteration has not warped the moral welfare of the inhabitants'.

Of the towns whose history is mainly summed up in

terms of trade, Halifax has some interests apart in antiquities and association with men of celebrity. Once it lay in the midst of forest glades and purling streams, a scene so serenely beautiful that it drew forth the rhapsody of 'Oh for a thousand tongues to sing' from a fervid spectator. Here, in his young manhood, was an organist in the parish church whose name, William Herschel, was eventually to resound as the discoverer of a wonder in space when a new planet swam into his ken, as the cataloguer of nebulae and star-clusters, and as the first President of the Astronomical Society. In Haughend parish Archbishop Tillotson was born, and in Sowerby Chapel his statue stands; the historian Sir Henry Saville, who founded the Professorship of Geology and Astronomy at Oxford, was a native of Bradley; John Foster, minister and essayist, belonged to Wadsworth, where the forbears of Longfellow are traced; and William Dearden was the poet of the region as his *Vale of Caldine* and *Star Seer* testify. In the town itself long dwelt George Hogarth, and for a little while John Collier, the Tim Bobbin of dialect fame, had employment at 'a desk's dull wood'.

In the days of George the Second Defoe reported in his Tour that Halifax was 'a compact sort of village with hardly an house standing out of a speaking distance from one another', and every house was a 'tenter', and every tenter had a piece of cloth. Long and bitterly did the weavers in this part of the country resist, even to the shedding of blood, the introduction of time-saving and wage-reducing innovations, and Charlotte Brontë in *Shirley* was able to turn to dramatic account the riots of '26, when the Bradford men opposed the power-loom, broke the accursed machines, and risked life and limb in a mad but vain effort to stem the progress of invention. Halifax has one claim to notoriety which may be hurriedly passed by, for there is no need to dilate on the Beggars' and Vagrants' Litany; suffice it that in the bad old times Hull was deemed 'terrible' by beggars, and Halifax 'formidable'. The notorious Gibbet, the mound of which can still be seen, dates back to Norman times, when an ordinance was made that a felon, who had taken goods valued by four constables at thirteen pence halfpenny, should be beheaded on market-day by a special 'engine' which anticipated the French guillotine. Taylor, the Water Poet, had a reference to this 'jyn' that

> wondrous quicke and well
> Sends thieves all headless into heaven or hell,

and there we may leave the unattractive subject.

'The largest city in the largest county in the country which has the largest empire', is the description which has been applied to that most paradoxical of places, Sheffield, a city of which much that is contradictory may be said, and all the contradictions be right; to get at the truth we must balance one with the other. We find Horace Walpole writing in 1760: 'I passed through Sheffield, which is one of the foulest towns in England in the most charming situation; there are two and twenty thousand inhabitants making knives and scissors: they remit eleven thousand pounds a week to London. One man there has discovered the art of plating copper with silver; I bought a pair of candlesticks for two guineas that are quite pretty.' We find Cobbett writing seventy years later: 'All the way along from Leeds to Sheffield it is coal and iron, and iron and coal. It was dark before we reached Sheffield; so that we saw the iron furnaces in all the horrible splendour of their everlasting blaze. Nothing can be conceived more grand or more terrific than the yellow waves of fire that incessantly issue from the top of these furnaces, some of which are close by the way-side.' After describing the process of combination, he went on: 'This Sheffield, and the land all about it, is one bed of iron and coal. They call it black Sheffield, and black enough it is; but from this one town and its environs go nine-tenths of the knives that are used in the whole world. If the people of Sheffield could only receive a tenth part of what their knives sell for by retail in America, Sheffield might pave its streets with silver.'

The aspect of Sheffield does not suggest romance. Encircled by hills, it lies in a gloomy hollow usually under a blanket of smoke. The view improves when the city is entered; the improvement increases in the environs, and the straggling streets wind upward to parks and groves of unimagined charm. Few thronged and busy work-centres, with clang and clatter, with furnaces and chimneys, with shops and factories, with miles of thoroughfares darkened with dingy tenements, have so delightful a setting—'a ring of emerald and amethyst'. On the Derbyshire side are the abrupt heights, the heather-tufted moors, the deep brooding woods, the vales of delicious verdure; streams ripple along their shining course and break into silvery cascades; the roads broaden and curve under long avenues of stately trees and reach out to old-world villages with gardens rich in bloom and lavish in colour. They may be just beyond the border, but are none the less the city suburbs. 'Smoky Sheffield' is the congested working hive, but there is another, spacious and opulent, where nature still bares her unspoiled beauty to the light.

And it is a city that, despite handicaps, has made much of opportunities. Taking the Cathedral as a centre, we see buildings of magnitude and no ignoble style in the main streets, a finely proportioned Town Hall, a new City Hall in the making. Forty natural parks and recreation grounds are within a short journey, two of them fifty acres in extent. The University rises in mellow redness amid lovely foliage. Ramblers make their way to Beauchief Abbey, the pious foundation of a knight who wished to expiate his part in à Becket's murder. It was dedicated to the martyr, but its purpose was 'for the salvation of the soul of King Henry II, and all his children, and for the salvation of my soul, and the souls of my heirs and all my relations, and for the souls of my father, my mother, and my wife, and all my ancestors', which was decidedly comprehensive. Since 1180 this Abbey of Robert Fitz-Ranulph has been a landmark in a fair demesne, and the great tower, massive in ruin, bears impress of the original power and beauty of the structure.

Still among antiquities of moving significance we come to the Lodge known as the Sheffield Manor haunted by the wraiths of Cardinal Wolsey and the Queen of Scots. Built for pleasure and repose by the Earl of Shrewsbury, Lord of Sheffield (*Gallorum terror, Sephilæus heros*: 'Gaul's terror, Sheffield's hero'), it was made the temporary prison of the fallen prelate, and within the same walls Queen Mary languished and was carried from room to room until her escape. Much of the story of her later days is concentrated here. Elizabeth had chosen Talbot of Shrewsbury for a difficult and delicate task by reason of his wealth, loyalty, high position, and judgment. He brought his captive to the castle with thirty attendants, French and Scots, but 'I have hur sure inoughe,' he wrote to his sovereign when there was a rumour that she might secure release, 'and shall kepe hur for the cumyng of your Ma'te's comandement, ether quyke or ded.' The Queen's French secretary, Rollet, died the following year, and was buried in Sheffield; Talbot took charge of her papers, and the perfidious Nau succeeded to Rollet's place. Elizabeth was still full of fear and suspicion, and the castle was filled with spies. When a son was born to Talbot the Queen conveyed her 'mislykings' to having women and strangers in the house. It was at Sheffield Manor that Mary made her will, despairing of life and liberty.

But perhaps the more pathetic narrative is that of Wolsey, who passed from honour to disgrace, from pride to destruction. The Earl received him with embraces, and gave him hearty welcome 'in my poor Lodge, when I have longe desiered to see you', and the Lord Cardinal rejoiced 'that my chance is to come into the custodie of so noble a person whose approved honour and wisdome hath alwaies bene right well knowne to all noble estate'. Then the drama slowly and irrevocably deepens down. The mighty one who had fallen 'applied his prayers continuallie' and refused all pleasures; sickness befell him, the physicians were sent for, and with Shrewsbury's consent he rode to Nottingham, and it was not long before death overtook him. The last public service of the Earl was to raise an army against the insurgents who met at Doncaster to oppose the suppression of the monasteries, and he dispersed them without a battle.

Yet it might be contended that the real romance of Sheffield lies in the industry that gives its name a world-wide distinction. In the steel factories to-day there are wonders of achievement which seem to belong to the realm of the magician rather than of the mechanician. We can witness the dull heavy metal being converted into flashing and delicate forms, a roll of rough dark iron transmuted into the brightest and sharpest of blades, an incongruous lump reappearing as the daintiest of table cutlery. The fame of it all has come down since Chaucer's day, when 'a Sheffield thwytel bare he in his hose' was written of the Miller of Trompington and his 'whittle', or knife, in the *Canterbury Tales*. The craftsman is skilled of hand and artistic of taste, and 'Sheffield Made' has a renown which implies that the qualities have been brought to their consummate powers. The term was known to the Plantagenets, and was understood when the dagger, topped by a jewelled or beaded hilt, was drawn by the gallant for deadly use or vain display.

The preamble of the Statute of the Cutlers' Company bore witness three centuries ago to the dexterity of the men who put the best edge to the steel, and the claim is made that the instinct is inherited that the best edge shall be assured and the priceless hall-mark of 'Sheffield Made' remain unmarred. And it was Emerson, who, discussing English tenacity of purpose and patience in awaiting results, instanced the Sheffield knife-grinders. At a mill he had been shown the process of making razors, and was told there was no 'luck' in making good steel, that the men 'made no mistake and every blade in the hundred and the thousand was good'. This city of massive girders, huge wheels, mighty engines, miles of rail, heavy ingots plunged into the crucible of white-hot fires—this city of blazing furnaces and cyclopaean sheds—this city which provides the world with giants in steel for the roads and with fairy-like filagrees for a lady's boudoir—is as full of marvel as a city of the genii in the *Arabian Nights*.

There is still one more surprise in its situation, and its easily accessible charms; and the half-amusing words of an old enthusiast are worth recalling: 'Rome boasted of its seven hills, but Sheffield has seventy times seven, and its scenery is made up of woods, vales, slopes, and sparkling streams, which no other part of the land can out-rival.' And of its celebrities James Montgomery said there were four 'to be placed in the first rank of Britons', and he named Jonathan Salt in botany, Charles Sylvester in experimental philosophy, Joseph Hunter in antiquities, and Francis Chantry in sculpture.

The last has the most assured place, worthy as the others may be. He is one of a small group of Yorkshire artists of high fame. York saw the birth of a delicate child, John Flaxman, who was wont to watch his father at work as a figure moulder and to attempt to imitate him. At eleven he was rewarded with a prize of the Society for the Encouragement of Art; and at fifteen the Royal Academy's silver medal was his. He secured the friendship of Blake, who deemed him 'the dear sculptor of Eternity', and Wedgwood was his associate in the painting of porcelain. His illustrations of Dante, his mural designs in Westminster Abbey, and his monuments—one in the Lady Chapel of St. Peter's, Leeds—are the evidence of the varied and supreme gifts of the man who was the Royal Academy's first Professor of Sculpture.

Brother in art was Chantry, who began his working

life as a milk-boy, and whose first sculpture, a bust in marble, was placed in Sheffield parish church. The Chantry Bequest, which yields two thousand pounds annually for the Royal Academy, may have had its origin in the youth's first earning of ten guineas—a heartening thought in an age where so many creeds are cancelled and hopes withdrawn. A third lowly born genius in this cluster is William Etty of York, son of a miller, apprenticed to a printer, but devoted irrepressibly to art. In the churchyard of St. Olave is his tomb, with an elaborate inscription bearing testimony to his 'exalted genius' and his 'undeviating perseverance'. 'To promote its advancement in his beloved country,' the epitaph continues, 'he watched the progress of those engaged in its study with the most disinterested kindness. To a cultivated and highly poetical mind were united a cheerfulness and sweetness of disposition with great simplicity and urbanity of manners. He was richly endeared to all who knew him.'

It would be the merest commonplace to instance achievement in the face of difficulties, for that is the way of genius; but Yorkshire supplies examples which have their curious characteristics. In the hamlet of Foulby was born at the end of the seventeenth century a carpenter's son, John Harrison, who was to construct a chronometer, the instrument which navigators had so long needed. Spain and Holland, as well as England had offered prizes for such an invention, and when even Sir Christopher Wren failed, the mechanical genius of a humble dalesman gave it to the world. And what shall we think of Nicholas Sanderson, of Thurlstone, who lost his sight before he was two years of age, but had such a talent for mathematics that he rose to be Lucasian Professor of Mathematics at

12

Cambridge. It is recorded of him that he learnt his letters by passing his fingers over the gravestones at Penistone. Such stories from life impart a deep meaning to the familiar term of ' Yorkshire grit '.

CHAPTER XI

THE LORE OF THE LAND

A LITERARY pilgrimage through Yorkshire has a twofold interest. It brings us into contact with authors who were natives of the county or spent much of their life within its borders and felt the influence of its scenery and associations ; and it makes us acquainted with works which have Yorkshire as a background. Frequently do we find ourselves in the footsteps of Sir Walter Scott. In *Ivanhoe* he described the ' district of merry England watered by the Don ', where in the days of Richard Lion Heart a large forest extended ' covering the greater part of the hills and valleys which lie between Sheffield and the pleasant town of Doncaster '. It was the land of Wamba the jester and the holy clerk of Copmanhurst ; the home of Athelstan was at Conisborough Castle, and Temple Newsam, the ancient seat of the Knights Templars, was the Templestowe of the story.

Well might it be so, that mansion on the crest of a hill in which was born Lord Darnley, the husband of Mary Queen of Scots, and father of King James of England. Domesday Book has a record of the original home of the de Lacys, but the history more definitely begins six centuries ago with the arrest of Frater Godefridus de Arcubus, preceptor de Newsom, and other Templars, by the high sheriff, and the confiscation of the estate. Many are the changes that ensued, and the chronicles are besmirched with intrigue and crime, treachery and tragedy, familiar to all students of Tudor and Stuart times. The ghost of the ill-fated beautiful Queen pervades the place; her portrait and relics make it a pathetic shrine.

We come to Scott again at Kirkby Moorside, eight miles or so from Pickering in a valley traversed by the Dove, where in a house in the Market Square death overtook George Villiers, Duke of Buckingham, the 'Steenie' of *The Fortunes of Nigel*. He had brought his 'Court' to Helmsley Castle for a revel in country life on that fine height overlooking Helmsley town with the Rye flowing by and luxuriant woods at hand. Alexander Pope, writing some hard lines on Buckingham's death, did not fail to remind us that his own mother came of a Yorkshire family, daughter of William Turner, of Worsborough in the dale of the Don. One of a family of seventeen, she was forty years of age when she wedded a London linen draper, and their only child was destined to be 'the little spider who spun the brilliant webs of verse'. Scott meets us again at West Tanfield, where the Marmions had their stronghold and where may be seen their effigies and tombs in alabaster; and thence we pass on to the abbey of St. Hilda at Whitby and watch the gentle Clare in her retreat.

But it was Rokeby's 'turrets high, northward in the dawning seen', the home of that Sir Thomas, the high sheriff, who fought and fell on Bramham Moor in the hour of his victory over the Earl of Northumberland, Bolingbroke's foe, which caught his fancy most strongly. The old house had been held by the Rokeby family from the Conqueror's time; it was burned by the Scots after Bannockburn though it stood sixty miles from 'the debatable land'; and a new mansion, bearing the old name, had passed into the ownership

WEST TANFIELD

of John B. S. Morritt, whom Scott visited in 1809. He fell in love with the scenery where 'Greta flows to meet the Tees', and thought it one of the most enviable places he had ever seen for richness and luxuriance of vegetation, and for the variety of glen, torrent, and copse. Inspired by these scenes Scott wrote his poem three years later, sketching the river course near Eggleston Abbey, Mortham Tower, haunted by the ghost of a headless woman, and Brignall Banks below Scargill where the robbers' cave is located.

Although Scott invented a story for Rokeby, or was inspired by the scenes to draw a group of characters fitting for such environment, he found in the locality itself legends and traditions which suited his mood. His passing allusions to the mysterious Rere-cross at Stanmore and to the hunting of the Felon Sow by the Friars of Richmond (the subject of one of the few medieval romances of a humorous nature) show how he had saturated his mind with the lore of the district; while his assiduity in securing correct details is attested by Mr. Morritt, who relates how he took a long journey for the sole purpose of describing at first-hand and with fidelity a robbers' cave and an old church; the two rode out to the slate quarries of Brignall and the abbey, where the poet made notes of the flowers and herbs that grew round the crag where he intended to locate an adventure of Guy Denzil.

He cast his story in Cavalier and Roundhead times, the events following immediately on the disaster at Marston Moor. Scott inhaled the very atmosphere of the region dominated by Rokeby Castle and Barnard Castle, and conjured up characters to fit a wild drama which might have come from Schiller's brain. His depiction of the river and the woodlands, and of scenes in morning freshness and evening flush, has been ranked among his most vividly beautiful ; praise to the verge of extravagance, though not fully endorsed by later generations, was once lavished upon it ; and the graphic description of the fire at Rokeby was perhaps more justly pronounced as unsurpassed of its kind. Not that the poem was among the popular successes, and Scott attributed this to the fact that Cavalier and Roundhead strife lacked the fascination of the theme of the primitive Highlanders. Public taste was changing, and a new influence was entering poetry ; if the publication of *Rokeby* were notable for nothing else it would be epoch-marking to the student of literature by its hailing of a greater bard by one who had been chief, the rival and conqueror who had arisen in Byron and to whose genius first place was graciously surrendered.

Yet Scott underestimated the hold that *Rokeby* would sustain upon lovers of poetic narrative, nor did he foresee that a hundred years later there would be many to find enchantment in the scene for his sake, and repeat with conviction that Brignall's Banks are wild and fair and Greta woods are green :

> And you may gather garlands there
> Would grace a summer queen.

A peep of the Hall is obtained by travelling along

> The stern and lone yet lovely road
> As e'er the foot of minstrel trode ;

and the far-spreading woods, the ravine through which the river rolls and then passes the old border-peel of Mortham, and the whole romantic setting, require no other artistry than the poet's words. The grassy slopes, the grey limestone, the flinty pathways, the chafing waters, gave him an exhilarating delight in the morning radiance and in the tranquil glow of evening : he loved every passing phase, every tint displayed :

> Here trees to every crevice clung,
> And o'er the dell their branches hung ;
> And there, all splinter'd and uneven,
> The shiver'd rocks ascend to heaven ;
> Oft, too, the ivy swath'd their breast,
> And wreath'd its garland round their crest ;
> Or from the spires bade loosely flare
> Its tendrils in the middle air,
> As pennons wont to wave of old
> O'er the high feast of Baron bold.

In these scenes he placed the figures of Matilda and her lover, the heroine, as he confessed, ' drawn from a lady who is no more ', that first love of his who remained an ideal to the last. Perhaps all this serves to add to the note of pathos in the thought of the devastation of Rokeby by fire, for the blast and ruin are depicted in a tumult of personal emotion :

> Through storied lattices no more
> In soften'd light the sunbeams pour,
> Gilding the Gothic sculpture rich
> Of shrine, and monument, and niche.

And mournfully the scene is left, a blackened mound in which the passing peasant vainly strives to trace the well-remembered symmetry and vanished splendour of the past.

Curious and detached segments of lore, legend, and history, like splinters chipped from graven tablets, lie scattered throughout the county. On one the name of Falstaff figures as owner of the Bentley estates ; on another is Guy Fawkes of Escrick Hall. The grim story of Walter Calverley's murder of two of his children, and his attempt upon his wife and a third child, was turned into a ballad, and made the plot of an Elizabethan drama, *The Yorkshire Tragedy*, attributed to George Wilkins with possibly a few lines from Shakespeare's hand. In Rossington Church was buried the king of the northern vagrants, Charles Bosvile (was his descendant the Flaming Tinman ?), a gentleman of some estate, but 'a mad spark who ran about the county', and made such friends with his kin, the gipsies, that they honoured his memory by pouring libations of hot ale on his grave.

Holy Church contributed stories of marvel, and one of Bolton Abbey, Saint Cuthbert, and Scrope will be found among the extravagant humours of the *Ingoldsby Legends*. Wordsworth, who was married at Brompton some little way from Scarborough, not only poetized the *White Doe of Rylstone* but the story of the chase which took place some five miles from Richmond near the small spring of water, Hart-Leap Well. 'The Knight had ridden down from Wensley Moor', and the pleasure-house he built served as monument to the gallant brute he had hunted to death. Long afterwards the poet, 'as I from Hawes to Richmond did repair', beheld the house in ruin, the land waste ; and his moral inevitably came :

> This beast not unobserved by Nature fell;
> His death was mourn'd by sympathy divine.

Such are a few oddments to be gathered as the pilgrim fares forth.

But of all the filaments of tradition there are none,

despite their fragility, more persistent than those of Robin Hood, *mitissimus praedonum*, the gentlest thief, most beloved of vagabonds. The conviction is almost forced upon us that Sherwood Forest extended to the South Riding, or even to Whitby, as a note in *Ivanhoe* has it, and that the merry men wandered freely over the dales. Nothing is too large or too small to associate with the band, whether a bay or a well, a hill or a boulder; and the wild woods echo to his name. There are huge stone seats on which he rested while pondering the next pleasant raid; there are rocks over which he vaulted; there are pools where he slaked his thirst; and there is a Pennystone at Luddenden, a trifle of solid granite, which he pitched from hill to hill for sheer amusement. He fought the Curtil Friar beside a well at Fountains, and at Skelbrook the men in green held their sports. Near Whitby Lathes stand two upright stones which we now know are none other than the arrows of Robin Hood and Little John, discharged by them from the top of the abbey, a mile and a half away, as a trial of strength—sure proof that in those days they drew the long bow.

The outlaw's renown intermingles with an adventure of a London merchant, Alderman Philpot, who fitted out an armed fleet to cope with the freebooter Mercer who had dashed into Scarborough harbour and carried off several vessels. Philpot's fleet pursued him and recaptured the ships together with several richly-laden Spanish vessels, and the exploit so fired popular imagination that it was sung in ballads; but the fame of Philpot was transferred to the hero of the forest. This was the easier because fancy already traced him to the bay which bore his name, and to the tumuli on Stoupe Brow where he and Little John and Scarlett had their butts. Sceptical archaeologists declare that the mounds are British or Danish, but does not their existence lend verisimilitude to an otherwise bald and unconvincing narrative? Yorkshire even contests with other counties the proud possession of Robin Hood's grave, on a hill, of which 'the people talk to this day', between Huddersfield and Dewsbury.

A more circumstantial story takes us to Kirklees, up the valley of the Calder, where the prioress, his aunt, bled him to death when he was distempered with cold and age. He had just enough strength to blow his bugle-horn, else Little John would never have reached him, taken revenge on the treacherous nunnery, and received his last wishes as to 'where his grave should diggèd be'. A block of stone on Kirklees glades, with the date of 1247, which antiquaries decline to certify as genuine, records the death of the Earl of Huntingdon, and by his side is his bent bow which once 'made music sweet':

> Let me have length and breadth enough,
> With a green sod under my head,
> That they may say when I am dead,
> There lies bold Robin Hood.

The father of English song, Caedmon, ploughman and poet, chanting his verse at Whitby, and putting into it somewhat of the roar of the northern winds, and Alcuin, exercising his scholarly influence from York, are two starry names in dim eras. Unknown ballad-makers come intermittently into the early story, some celebrating heroes and battles, some favouring a long-drawn tale of a dragon at Wantley, or otherwise Wharncliffe:

> In Yorkshire, near fair Rotherham,
> The place I know it well. . . .

There is a hedge, just on the hill-edge,
And Matthew's house hard by it,
O, there and then was this dragon's den,
You could not chuse but spy it

—the rambling and mythical narrative probably embodying the history of a local contest connected with a Wortley enclosure or some other legal disputation. The mention of the family who had their domain in the region of the Crags, serves also to recall famous, witty, letter-writing Lady Mary, who by marriage brought new lustre to the name; and though she had little enough to interest her in the locality, there are occasionally references in her correspondence with her husband which link her to the county: 'There is a house five miles from York, extremely well furnished and every way proper for us'; 'If you persist in your silence I will return to Wharncliffe'; 'I can't forbear entertaining you with our York lovers'; 'The Archbishop of York has been come to Bishopthorpe but three days, and I went with my cousin to see the King proclaimed (August 9th 1714) which was done; the Archbishop walking next the Lord Mayor, all the county gentry following, with greater crowds of people than I believed to be in York, vast acclamations, and a general satisfaction—the Pretender afterwards dragged about the streets and burned'. It was the lady's ambition that her husband 'should be chose for York, if declared in time', and she deplored that he should enter Parliament by buying some little borough: ''Tis a surprise to me that you cannot make sure when so many insignificant creatures come in without any opposition.'

Closer to the locality, although he was not a native, was a writer of after-times, James Montgomery, whom

Leigh Hunt, with somewhat rash generosity, welcomed to his *Feast of Poets* as one whom Apollo honoured by the side of Shelley, Keats, and Byron ; but in so doing he was paying high tribute to the man's personal worth as much as to his talent. Long and tedious poems are redeemed by admirable lines, such as those on Home, which shine out amid the arid waste of his epic on *The West Indies* ; and of his hundred hymns so many have kept their place and exercised their influence despite familiarity that we must regard him as one of the most successful practitioners in this difficult medium. Montgomery lives in his sacred songs, and through them continues to reach thousands of hearts. It surprises us to know that so gentle a man, with lofty ideals on purity and freedom, was twice cast into prison ; but he lived in days when exalted opinion was dangerous if it were opposed to orthodoxy and authority. His first offence was 'sedition'—his journal had printed a ballad on the fall of the Bastille ; and his second offence was 'libel'—he had dared to criticize a magistrate's conduct in the quelling of a riot in Sheffield. A volume of poems devoted to *Prison Amusements* was the result of these experiences. Could Montgomery have been relieved of the daily drudgery of journalism (he was editor and proprietor of the *Sheffield Iris*) he might have winged his flights higher. His last years were tranquil, his good life finished when he was eighty-three ; he enjoyed a fame which has inevitably declined, and a tablet to his memory looks down on the visitor to the Cutlers' Hall.

Ebenezer Elliott, the Sheffield ironfounder and Corn-Law rhymester, was something of a kindred spirit, but more fiery and impassioned. Before Cobden and Bright began the long and ardent campaign for Free

Trade, Elliott was preparing the way and denouncing the Bread Tax. His verses had an infectious strain, and the multitude caught his anger at evil and his enthusiasm for reform :

> On these pale lips the smothered thought
> Which England's millions feel,
> A fierce and fearful splendour caught,
> As from his forge, the steel.

So Whittier wrote in his requiem. But Elliott's poetic fervour was not wholly devoted to political campaigning. He had a deep love for nature, and he painted in such true and striking colours the beauty lying around him that many there are who instinctively respond to his *Poet's Prayer* and are 'pleased to read his lays', and love, for his sake, 'the scenes where he hath been'.

One other Yorkshire author of repute must have brief mention, Charles Waterton, foremost among field naturalists and author of that romantic, exciting, and informing classic *Wanderings in America*, who bequeathed his wondrous collection to Ushaw College, Durham, and Stonyhurst College, Lancashire. At his home at Walton Hall, near Wakefield, he had the advantage of facilities to study wild life. He made a sanctuary of his grounds, waging war only on the brown rat, likening it unto the Hanoverians, whom, like a Jacobite and Catholic, he hated. If he were remembered for nothing else, schoolboys would cherish his memory for the sake of one wild adventure when, threatened with death, he sprang upon the back of a hooked monster cayman, or alligator, and triumphantly rode it out of the river in good fox-hunting style, where it was dispatched. His grim humour was displayed in the horrent objects he fashioned out of parts of animals. To one he gave the name of his special aversion, Luther; while another was supposed to represent John Bull suffering under the heavy weight of the National Debt piled on his back in plethoric bags!

The fields of literature and art must be accounted rich when from them sprang men like Porteous, whose poems had such vogue in his day; William Stubbs, whose historical studies brought him high and numerous academic honours; George Gissing, who from Wakefield went out into the world to wage a hard fight for the recognition of his genius; Silvanus Thompson, physicist, author, and lecturer; Mary Linskill, who wrote *Between the Heather and the Northern Sea*; and Halliwell Sutcliffe, who is the incomparable word-painter of the moors. His Yorkshire, it has been aptly said, is a county where loves and fears go deep, where trolls and the ghostly hound of legend are remembered as very real things, and where men live close to nature's heart of mystery and dread. It is to him the land of potters and gipsies, farmers and yeomen, shepherds and drovers, free and keen-witted dalesmen.

Such writers do not lack curious materials for their stories—they can summon up strange figures of the past or recall custom and tradition of perpetual interest. Dickens might have culled another Poor Travellers' romance at Sprotborough, which afforded special hospitality to men on the lonely highway to Mexborough, a stone pillar in 1520 bearing the cordial invitation:

> Whoso is hungry and list well eate,
> Let him come to Spotburgh to his meate,

with a promise that he could stay a day and a night and be asked no questions on departure.

Or how amazing it would have been to converse with patriarchal Jenkins of Swaledale, whose monument declares that his life was spun out to one hundred and sixty-nine years, and that he remembered much that occurred between 1500 and 1669. He might have been a pleasant old crony for Drunken Barnaby, otherwise Richard Braithwaite, who has his monument in Catterick Church, but whose queer rhymings on his seventeenth-century tour have made his name a household word. And was not Robinson Crusoe himself a Yorkshireman? If his chronicler is to be trusted he was 'born in the year 1632, in the city of York, of a good family, though not of that county, my father being a foreigner of Bremen, named Kreutznaer, who settled first at Hull'—as the opening sentence in the immortal work of adventure informs us. And as the father migrated to York, and the mother was 'of a very good family in that county', no further evidence is surely required to establish the claim.

It is a little surprising that Harrison Ainsworth, whose Rookwood Park was only half an hour's sharp riding from the Don, did not in the course of his researches come upon a fanatic who might have figured strikingly in his historical romances. The bigotry of an age of extremists has produced few weirder creatures than John Saltmarshe, who traced his descent back to Saxon times, but was cast into the midst of a century when religious zeal ran to madness. He was born at Healeston, near Malton, entered the Church, turned Presbyterian, then joined the Calvinists. But after serving as chaplain in Fairfax's army he convinced himself that monarchies were for ever ended and that the second coming of Christ was at hand, when a kingdom of saints would be established and endure a thousand years. He preached with fervour, he wrote in poetry and prose, he engaged in fiery controversy although 'love and peace' were his favourite themes. A list of the titles of his books creates amusement: *Perfume against the Sulphurus Stinke of the Snuff of the 'Light for Smoak' called 'Novello-Mastrix', with a check to Cerbero-Diabolus and a Whip for his barking against the Parliament and the Armie*, may serve as a specimen, and it is to be hoped that a would-be purchaser remembered what to ask for.

After the battle of Naseby, Saltmarshe turned prophet and had supernatural visions and 'extatical raptures'. In a trance he was borne to heaven, where he found there was much concern as to Cromwell's designs, and he was told to deliver a divine message to the army. On returning to earth he set about fulfilling his mission, rode to Windsor, commanded the troops to depart from their tents lest they perish, and went on 'with the spirit of a lion' to interview the lieutenant-general himself. 'The Lord is angry with you,' said he, 'for causing godly men to be imprisoned, slighted, and abused', with much more of an outright character, and Cromwell 'wondered to hear such passages fall from his lips', but let him go his way. And away the fanatic went, got home, composedly ate and slept, and then announced to his wife that he would die next day. The following morning he was speechless, and in the afternoon his prophecy was fulfilled.

The romancer could likewise let his fancy roam round the garden region of Cropton, where William Scoresby, sea-captain, explorer, scientist, author, clergyman, spent his dreary youth; or should he require a truly spacious scene wherein to set a sumptuous pageant, no finer choice could be desired than Wentworth Woodhouse, with its encircling park of eight miles, the classically designed edifice stately with Ionic pillars, and itself the largest private house the world knows. Even the stabling is on a huge scale, and any proud possessor of a hundred and fifty horses would find ample accommodation for them. Inside this lordly dwelling are masterpieces of art, pictures by Vandyck, Teniers, Titian, da Vinci, Raphael, Reynolds, and Lely. The name of Wentworth supplies the clue to the mystery that here are treasured the veritable Bible and Prayer Book of the martyred King, and that Strafford's oak billiard table is also to be seen. But this would be 'matter for another tale'.

But as we recall fact and myth, events far-off or near, the multitudinous details of a great epic, we feel that the story of Yorkshire, like its extent, is so vast that we do but touch the fringes. The one hope must be that we have been led toward a goal and may march on expectant of more reward.

BY WAY OF EPILOGUE

History, legend, romance, phantasms of the past, are the immaterialities out of which is wrought the spell that binds us to Place. This is the only witchcraft needful for use to bring forth the enchantment of scenery in brightness or in shadow, that scenery which once served for drama, for stirring event, for pageantry and the procession of great figures. The air kindles with memories. If the spell still has power the scenes break upon the vision with a new glamour, that undefinable sensation when a picture is so mysteriously irradiated as to arouse a feeling of enchantment, when the spirit quickens, and when memory stores an impression never to be effaced. These are the moments of wonder when 'the ivory gates fall back at the fairy touch', and the kingdom of romance is revealed. Glamour, in such times of emotion, means both vision and illusion, reality and dream—it is a spell when those forms that are beheld

> Come apparell'd in more precious habit,
> More moving-delicate, and full of life,
> Into the eye and prospect of the soul.

To describe such glamour would be to destroy it—'magic would not be magic if it could be explained'. All we know is that we experience it when the blue haze hangs upon the moors, when the evening ray softly illumines a shrine, when the sunlight mellows rugged castle ruins and the 'golden stain of time' shows upon the antique stones, or when cathedral towers standing out against a clear sky inscribe a poem

THE CASTLE OF THE SCROPES

expressive of the reverence of the great designers. The poets have interpreted the mysteries, and have caught up the legends and traditions clinging to the haunts of loveliness; and in the wild moorlands the romancers have found eerie suggestion or conjured up fearsome figures for their dramas. The spell worked irresistibly, and in these pages we have sought to trace where and how.

INDEX

PRINTED BY
JARRALD AND SONS LTD.
NORWICH

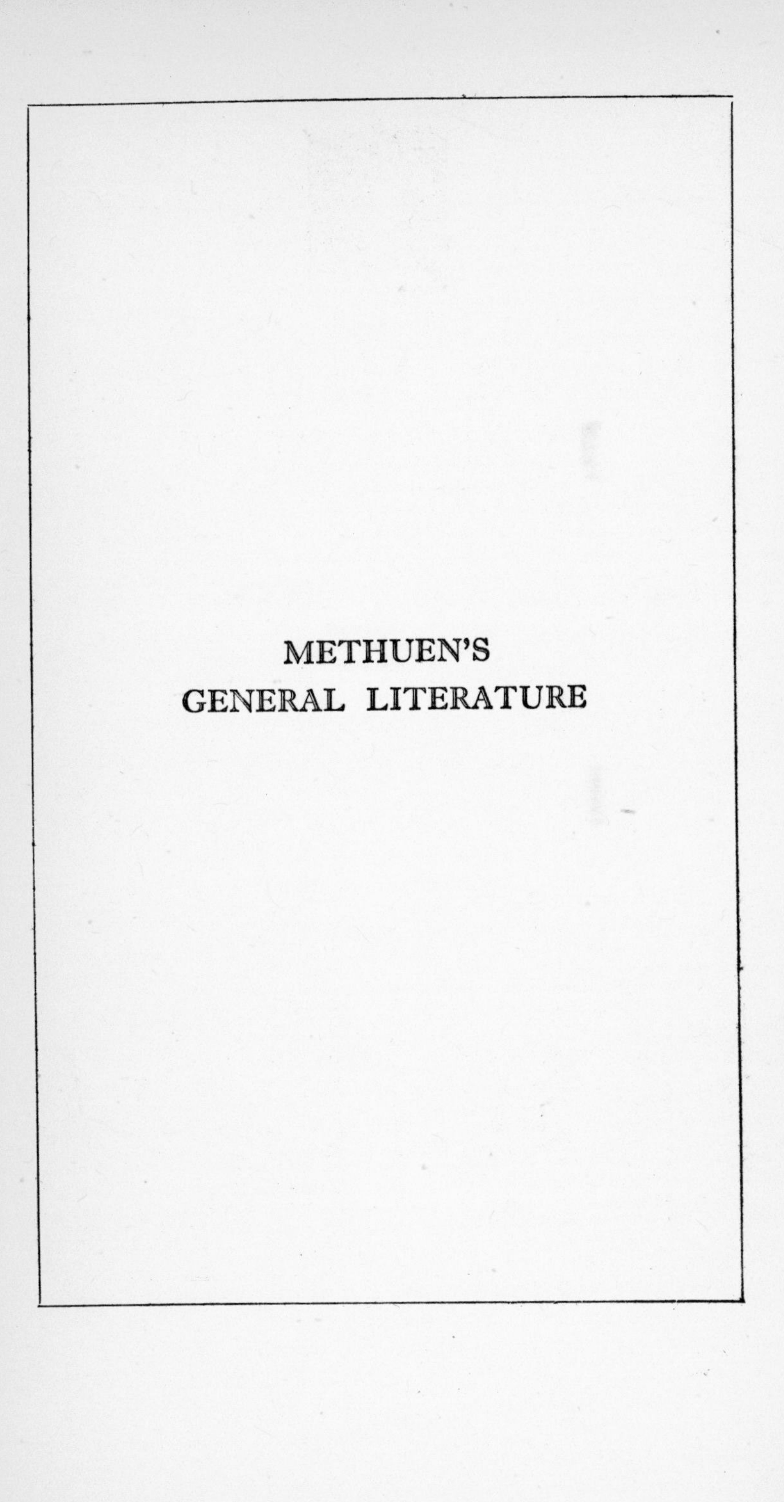

METHUEN'S
GENERAL LITERATURE

BIRMINGHAM (George A.)
A WAYFARER IN HUNGARY
Illustrated. 8*s.* 6*d.* *net.*
SPILLIKINS: ESSAYS 3*s.* 6*d.* *net.*
SHIPS AND SEALING-WAX: ESSAYS
3*s.* 6*d.* *net.*

BUDGE (Sir E. A. Wallis)
A HISTORY OF ETHIOPIA: NUBIA AND ABYSSINIA
Illustrated. 2 vols. £3 13*s.* 6*d.* *net.*

CHESTERTON (G. K.)
COME TO THINK OF IT . . .
6*s.* *net.*
G.K.C. AS M.C. 7*s.* 6*d.* *net.*
THE BALLAD OF THE WHITE HORSE
3*s.* 6*d.* *net.*
Also Illustrated by ROBERT AUSTIN. 12*s.* 6*d.* *net.*
CHARLES DICKENS
GENERALLY SPEAKING
ALL THINGS CONSIDERED
TREMENDOUS TRIFLES
FANCIES VERSUS FADS
ALARMS AND DISCURSIONS
A MISCELLANY OF MEN
THE USES OF DIVERSITY
THE OUTLINE OF SANITY
THE FLYING INN
Each 3*s.* 6*d.* *net.*
A GLEAMING COHORT 2*s.* 6*d.* *net.*
WINE, WATER AND SONG
1*s.* 6*d.* *net.*

CLUTTON-BROCK (A.)
WHAT IS THE KINGDOM OF HEAVEN?
ESSAYS ON ART
SHAKESPEARE'S HAMLET
Each 5*s.* *net.*
MORE ESSAYS ON BOOKS
ESSAYS ON RELIGION
MORE ESSAYS ON RELIGION
Each 6*s.* *net.*
SHELLEY, THE MAN AND THE POET
Illustrated. 7*s.* 6*d.* *net.*
ESSAYS ON BOOKS
ESSAYS ON LITERATURE AND LIFE
ESSAYS ON LIFE *Each* 3*s.* 6*d.* *net.*

CRAWLEY (Ernest)
THE MYSTIC ROSE. Revised and Enlarged by THEODORE BESTERMAN. 2 vols. £1 10*s.* *net.*
STUDIES OF SAVAGES AND SEX
Edited by THEODORE BESTERMAN.
10*s.* 6*d.* *net.*
DRESS, DRINKS AND DRUMS. Edited by THEODORE BESTERMAN. 12*s.* 6*d.* *net.*

DUGDALE (E. T. S.)
GERMAN DIPLOMATIC DOCUMENTS, 1871–1914
Selected from the Documents published by the German Foreign Office. In 4 vols. Vol. I, 1871–90. Vol. II, 1891–8. Vol. III, 1898–1910. Vol. IV, 1911–1914.
Each £1 1*s.* *net.*

EDWARDES (Tickner)
THE LORE OF THE HONEY-BEE
Illustrated. 7*s.* 6*d.* and 3*s.* 6*d.* *net.*
BEEKEEPING FOR ALL
Illustrated. 3*s.* 6*d.* *net.*
THE BEE-MASTER OF WARRILOW
Illustrated. 7*s.* 6*d.* *net.*
BEE-KEEPING DO'S AND DONT'S
2*s.* 6*d.* *net.*
LIFT-LUCK ON SOUTHERN ROADS
Illustrated. 5*s.* *net.*

EINSTEIN (Albert)
RELATIVITY: THE SPECIAL AND GENERAL THEORY 5*s.* *net.*
SIDELIGHTS ON RELATIVITY
3*s.* 6*d.* *net.*
THE MEANING OF RELATIVITY
5*s.* *net.*
THE BROWNIAN MOVEMENT
5*s.* *net.*

EISLER (Robert)
THE MESSIAH JESUS AND JOHN THE BAPTIST: according to Flavius Josephus' recently rediscovered 'Capture of Jerusalem' and the other Jewish and Christian sources. Translated by A. HAGGERTY KRAPPE.
Illustrated. *Demy 8vo.* £2 2*s.* *net.*

FIELD (G. C.)
MORAL THEORY 6*s.* *net.*
PLATO AND HIS CONTEMPORARIES
12*s.* 6*d.* *net.*

FYLEMAN (Rose)
FAIRIES AND CHIMNEYS
THE FAIRY GREEN
THE FAIRY FLUTE
THE RAINBOW CAT
EIGHT LITTLE PLAYS FOR CHILDREN
FORTY GOOD-NIGHT TALES
FAIRIES AND FRIENDS
THE ADVENTURE CLUB
FORTY GOOD-MORNING TALES
SEVEN LITTLE PLAYS FOR CHILDREN
TWENTY TEA-TIME TALES
Each 3*s.* 6*d.* *net.*

FYLEMAN (Rose)—*continued*
THE DOLLS' HOUSE
Illustrated by MARGARET TEMPEST.
5*s. net.*
GAY GO UP
Illustrated by DECIE MERWIN.
5*s. net.*
THE ROSE FYLEMAN FAIRY BOOK
Illustrated by HILDA MILLER.
10*s.* 6*d. net.*
A GARLAND OF ROSES: COLLECTED POEMS
Illustrated by RENÉ BULL.
8*s.* 6*d. net.*

GIBBON (Edward)
THE DECLINE AND FALL OF THE ROMAN EMPIRE
With Notes, Appendixes and Maps, by J. B. BURY. Illustrated. 7 vols. *Demy* 8*vo.* 15*s. net* each volume. Also, unillustrated. *Crown* 8*vo.* 7*s.* 6*d. net* each volume.

GLADSTONE (Mary) (Mrs. Drew)
HER DIARIES AND LETTERS
Illustrated. £1 1*s. net.*

GLOVER (T. R.)
VIRGIL
THE CONFLICT OF RELIGIONS IN THE EARLY ROMAN EMPIRE
POETS AND PURITANS
Each 10*s.* 6*d. net.*
FROM PERICLES TO PHILIP
12*s.* 6*d. net.*

GRAHAM (Harry)
THE WORLD WE LAUGH IN: More Deportmental Ditties
Illustrated by 'FISH'. *Eighth Edition.* 5*s. net.*
STRAINED RELATIONS
Illustrated by H. STUART MENZIES and HENDY. 6*s. net.*
THE WORLD'S WORKERS
Illustrated by 'FOUGASSE'.
5*s. net.*
ADAM'S APPLES
Illustrated by JOHN REYNOLDS.
5*s. net.*

GRAHAME (Kenneth)
THE WIND IN THE WILLOWS
207*th Thousand.* 7*s.* 6*d. net.*
Also illustrated by WYNDHAM PAYNE. 7*s.* 6*d. net.*
Also unillustrated.
Cloth; 3*s.* 6*d. net.*
Green Morocco, 7*s.* 6*d. net.*
See also **Milne (A. A.)**

HADFIELD (J. A.)
PSYCHOLOGY AND MORALS
Eighth Edition. Crown 8*vo.* 6*s. net.*

HALL (H. R.)
THE ANCIENT HISTORY OF THE NEAR EAST
Illustrated. £1 1*s. net.*
THE CIVILIZATION OF GREECE IN THE BRONZE AGE
Illustrated. £1 10*s. net.*
A SEASON'S WORK AT UR OF THE CHALDEES. Illustrated. £1 5*s. net.*

HEATON (Rose Henniker)
THE PERFECT HOSTESS
Decorated by A. E. TAYLOR.
7*s.* 6*d. net.* Gift Edition, £1 1*s. net.*

HERBERT (A. P.)
HONEYBUBBLE & CO. 6*s. net.*
MISLEADING CASES IN THE COMMON LAW. With an Introduction by LORD HEWART. 5*s. net.*
MORE MISLEADING CASES 5*s. net.*
WISDOM FOR THE WISE
Illustrated by GEORGE MORROW.
5*s. net.*
THE WHEREFORE AND THE WHY
Illustrated by GEORGE MORROW.
3*s.* 6*d. net.*
THE BOMBER GIPSY 3*s.* 6*d. net.*
THE SECRET BATTLE 3*s.* 6*d. net.*
TANTIVY TOWERS 2*s.* 6*d. net.*
MR. MAFFERTY 5*s. net.*

HOLDSWORTH (Sir W. S.)
A HISTORY OF ENGLISH LAW
Nine Volumes. £1 5*s. net each.*

HUDSON (W. H.)
A SHEPHERD'S LIFE
Illustrated. 10*s.* 6*d. net.*
Also unillustrated. 3*s.* 6*d. net.*

HUTTON (Edward)
CITIES OF SICILY
Illustrated. 10*s.* 6*d. net.*
MILAN AND LOMBARDY
THE CITIES OF ROMAGNA AND THE MARCHES
SIENA AND SOUTHERN TUSCANY
NAPLES AND SOUTHERN ITALY
Illustrated. *Each* 8*s.* 6*d. net.*
A WAYFARER IN UNKNOWN TUSCANY
THE CITIES OF SPAIN
THE CITIES OF UMBRIA
COUNTRY WALKS ABOUT FLORENCE
ROME
FLORENCE AND NORTHERN TUSCANY
VENICE AND VENETIA
Illustrated. *Each* 7*s.* 6*d. net.*

INGE (W. R.), D.D., Dean of St. Paul's
CHRISTIAN MYSTICISM
(The Bampton Lectures of 1899).
Sixth Edition. 7*s.* 6*d. net.*

KIPLING (Rudyard)
BARRACK-ROOM BALLADS
255th Thousand.
THE SEVEN SEAS
186th Thousand.
THE FIVE NATIONS
143rd Thousand.
DEPARTMENTAL DITTIES
117th Thousand.
THE YEARS BETWEEN
95th Thousand.
Four Editions of these famous volumes of poems are now published, viz. :—
Crown 8vo. Buckram, 7*s.* 6*d. net.*
Fcap. 8vo. Cloth, 6*s. net.*
Leather 7*s.* 6*d. net.*
Service Edition. Two volumes each book. *Square Fcap. 8vo.* 3*s. net* each volume.
A KIPLING ANTHOLOGY—VERSE
Sixth Edition.
Leather 7*s.* 6*d. net.*
Cloth 6*s. net* and 3*s.* 6*d. net.*
TWENTY POEMS FROM RUDYARD KIPLING
486th Thousand. 1*s. net.*
A CHOICE OF SONGS
Second Edition. 2*s. net.*

LAISTNER (M. L. W.)
THOUGHT AND LETTERS IN WESTERN EUROPE (A.D. 500–900). 15*s. net.*

LAMB (Charles and Mary)
THE COMPLETE WORKS
Edited by E. V. LUCAS. Six Volumes. With Frontispieces. 6*s. net each.*
SELECTED LETTERS
Edited by G. T. CLAPTON. 3*s.* 6*d. net.*
THE CHARLES LAMB DAY BOOK
Compiled by E. V. LUCAS. 6*s. net.*

LANKESTER (Sir Ray)
SCIENCE FROM AN EASY CHAIR
SCIENCE FROM AN EASY CHAIR : Second Series
DIVERSIONS OF A NATURALIST
GREAT AND SMALL THINGS
Illustrated. *Each* 7*s.* 6*d. net.*
SECRETS OF EARTH AND SEA
Illustrated. 8*s.* 6*d. net.*

LINDRUM (Walter)
BILLIARDS. Illustrated. 6*s. net.*

LODGE (Sir Oliver)
MAN AND THE UNIVERSE
7*s.* 6*d. net* and 3*s.* 6*d. net.*
THE SURVIVAL OF MAN
7*s.* 6*d. net.*
RAYMOND 10*s.* 6*d. net.*
RAYMOND REVISED 6*s. net.*
MODERN PROBLEMS 3*s.* 6*d. net.*
REASON AND BELIEF 3*s.* 6*d. net.*
THE SUBSTANCE OF FAITH
2*s. net.*
RELATIVITY 1*s. net.*
CONVICTION OF SURVIVAL 2*s. net.*

LUCAS (E. V.)
THE LIFE OF CHARLES LAMB
2 Vols. £1 1*s. net.*
THE COLVINS AND THEIR FRIENDS
£1 1*s. net.*
VERMEER THE MAGICAL 5*s. net.*
A WANDERER IN ROME
A WANDERER IN HOLLAND
A WANDERER IN LONDON
LONDON REVISITED (Revised)
A WANDERER IN PARIS
A WANDERER IN FLORENCE
A WANDERER IN VENICE
Each 10*s.* 6*d. net.*
A WANDERER AMONG PICTURES
8*s.* 6*d. net.*
E. V. LUCAS'S LONDON £1 *net.*
INTRODUCING LONDON
INTRODUCING PARIS
Each 2*s.* 6*d. net.*
THE OPEN ROAD 6*s. net.*
Also, illustrated by CLAUDE A. SHEPPERSON, A.R.W.S.
10*s.* 6*d. net.*
Also, India Paper.
Leather, 7*s.* 6*d. net.*
THE JOY OF LIFE
6*s. net. Leather Edition,* 7*s.* 6*d. net.*
Also, India Paper.
Leather, 7*s.* 6*d. net.*
THE GENTLEST ART 3*s.* 6*d. net.*
And THE SECOND POST 3*s.* 6*d. net.*
Also together in one volume.
7*s.* 6*d. net.*
FIRESIDE AND SUNSHINE
CHARACTER AND COMEDY
GOOD COMPANY
ONE DAY AND ANOTHER
OLD LAMPS FOR NEW
LOITERER'S HARVEST
LUCK OF THE YEAR
EVENTS AND EMBROIDERIES
A FRONDED ISLE
A ROVER I WOULD BE
GIVING AND RECEIVING
HER INFINITE VARIETY
ENCOUNTERS AND DIVERSIONS
TURNING THINGS OVER
Each 3*s.* 6*d. net.*

LUCAS (E. V.)—*continued*
CLOUD AND SILVER
A BOSWELL OF BAGHDAD
'TWIXT EAGLE AND DOVE
THE PHANTOM JOURNAL
ZIGZAGS IN FRANCE
TRAVELLER'S LUCK
VISIBILITY GOOD *Each* 6*s*. *net*.
FRENCH LEAVES
Illustrated. 5*s*. *net*.
ROVING EAST AND ROVING WEST 5*s*. *net*.
Mr. Punch's COUNTY SONGS
Illustrated by E. H. SHEPARD. 10*s*. 6*d*. *net*.
'THE MORE I SEE OF MEN . . .'
OUT OF A CLEAR SKY
IF DOGS COULD WRITE
'. . . AND SUCH SMALL DEER'
Each 3*s*. 6*d*. *net*.
THE PEKINESE NATIONAL ANTHEM
Illustrated by PERSIS KIRMSE. 1*s*. *net*.
See also **Lamb (Charles)**.

LYND (Robert)
IT'S A FINE WORLD 5*s*. *net*.
THE GREEN MAN
THE PLEASURES OF IGNORANCE
THE GOLDFISH
THE LITTLE ANGEL
THE BLUE LION
THE PEAL OF BELLS
THE MONEY-BOX
THE ORANGE TREE *Each* 3*s*. 6*d*. *net*.

McDOUGALL (William)
AN INTRODUCTION TO SOCIAL PSYCHOLOGY 10*s*. 6*d*. *net*.
NATIONAL WELFARE AND NATIONAL DECAY 6*s*. *net*.
AN OUTLINE OF PSYCHOLOGY 10*s*. 6*d*. *net*.
AN OUTLINE OF ABNORMAL PSYCHOLOGY 15*s*. *net*.
BODY AND MIND 12*s*. 6*d*. *net*.
CHARACTER AND THE CONDUCT OF LIFE 10*s*. 6*d*. *net*.
MODERN MATERIALISM AND EMERGENT EVOLUTION 7*s*. 6*d*. *net*.
ETHICS AND SOME MODERN WORLD PROBLEMS 7*s*. 6*d*. *net*.
A BRIEF OUTLINE OF PSYCHOLOGY: Normal and Abnormal
8*s*. 6*d*. *net*.

MALLET (Sir C. E.)
A HISTORY OF THE UNIVERSITY OF OXFORD
In 3 vols. *Each* £1 1*s*. *net*.

MAETERLINCK (Maurice)
THE BLUE BIRD 6*s*. *net*.
Also, illustrated by F. CAYLEY ROBINSON. 10*s*. 6*d*. *net*.
OUR ETERNITY 6*s*. *net*.
THE UNKNOWN GUEST 6*s*. *net*.
POEMS 5*s*. *net*.
THE WRACK OF THE STORM 6*s*. *net*.
THE BURGOMASTER OF STILEMONDE 5*s*. *net*.
THE BETROTHAL 6*s*. *net*.
MOUNTAIN PATHS 6*s*. *net*.
THE GREAT SECRET 7*s*. 6*d*. *net*.
THE CLOUD THAT LIFTED and THE POWER OF THE DEAD 7*s*. 6*d*. *net*.
MARY MAGDALENE 2*s*. *net*.

MARLOWE (Christopher)
THE WORKS. In 6 volumes.
General Editor, R. H. CASE.
THE LIFE OF MARLOWE, by C. F. TUCKER BROOKE, and DIDO. Edited by the Same. 8*s*. 6*d*. *net*.
TAMBURLAINE, I AND II. Edited by U. M. ELLIS-FERMOR. 10*s*. 6*d*. *net*.
THE JEW OF MALTA and THE MASSACRE AT PARIS
Edited by H. S. BENNETT. 10*s*. 6*d*. *net*.
POEMS
Edited by L. C. MARTIN. 10*s*. 6*d* *net*.

MASEFIELD (John)
ON THE SPANISH MAIN 8*s*. 6*d*. *net*.
A SAILOR'S GARLAND 3*s*. 6*d*. *net*.
SEA LIFE IN NELSON'S TIME 7*s*. 6*d*. *net*.

METHUEN (Sir A.)
AN ANTHOLOGY OF MODERN VERSE
232nd Thousand.
SHAKESPEARE TO HARDY: An Anthology of English Lyrics
28th Thousand.
Each, Cloth, 6*s*. *net*.
Leather, 7*s*. 6*d*. *net*.

MILNE (A. A.)
BY WAY OF INTRODUCTION 6*s*. *net*.
TOAD OF TOAD HALL
A Play founded on Kenneth Grahame's 'The Wind in the Willows.' 5*s*. *net*.
THOSE WERE THE DAYS: Collected Stories 7*s*. 6*d*. *net*.
NOT THAT IT MATTERS
IF I MAY
THE SUNNY SIDE
THE RED HOUSE MYSTERY
ONCE A WEEK
THE HOLIDAY ROUND

MILNE (A. A.)—*continued*
THE DAY'S PLAY
MR. PIM PASSES BY
Each 3*s*. 6*d*. *net*.
WHEN WE WERE VERY YOUNG
211*th Thousand*.
WINNIE-THE-POOH
118*th Thousand*.
NOW WE ARE SIX
119*th Thousand*.
THE HOUSE AT POOH CORNER
105*th Thousand*.
Each illustrated by E. H. SHEPARD.
7*s*. 6*d*. *net*. *Leather*, 10*s*. 6*d* *net*.
THE CHRISTOPHER ROBIN STORY BOOK. *Third Edition*.
Illustrated by E. H. SHEPARD.
5*s*. *net*.
THE CHRISTOPHER ROBIN BIRTHDAY BOOK
Illustrated by E. H. SHEPARD.
3*s*. 6*d*. *net*.

MILNE (A. A.) and FRASER-SIMSON (H.)
FOURTEEN SONGS FROM 'WHEN WE WERE VERY YOUNG'
Thirteenth Edition. 7*s*. 6*d*. *net*.
TEDDY BEAR AND OTHER SONGS FROM 'WHEN WE WERE VERY YOUNG' 7*s*. 6*d*. *net*.
THE KING'S BREAKFAST
Third Edition. 3*s*. 6*d*. *net*.
SONGS FROM 'NOW WE ARE SIX'
Second Edition. 7*s*. 6*d*. *net*.
MORE 'VERY YOUNG' SONGS
7*s*. 6*d*. *net*.
THE HUMS OF POOH 7*s*. 6*d*. *net*.
Words by A. A. MILNE.
Music by H. FRASER-SIMSON.
Decorations by E. H. SHEPARD.

MORTON (H. V.)
THE HEART OF LONDON
35*th Thousand*. 3*s*. 6*d*. *net*.
Also with Scissor Cuts by L. HUMMEL. 6*s*. *net*.
THE SPELL OF LONDON
25*th Thousand*.
THE NIGHTS OF LONDON
18*th Thousand*. *Each* 3*s*. 6*d*. *net*.
IN SEARCH OF ENGLAND
74*th Thousand*.
THE CALL OF ENGLAND
35*th Thousand*.
IN SEARCH OF SCOTLAND
96*th Thousand*.
IN SEARCH OF IRELAND
40*th Thousand*.
IN SEARCH OF WALES
Each illustrated. 7*s*. 6*d*. *net*.

NEUBURGER (Albert)
THE TECHNICAL ARTS AND SCIENCES OF THE ANCIENTS
Translated by H. L. BROSE.
Illustrated. £2 2*s*. *net*.

OMAN (Sir Charles)
A HISTORY OF THE ART OF WAR IN THE MIDDLE AGES, A.D. 378–1485
2 vols. Illustrated. £1 16*s*. *net*.
STUDIES IN THE NAPOLEONIC WARS
8*s*. 6*d*. *net*.

PERRY (W. J.)
THE ORIGIN OF MAGIC AND RELIGION
THE GROWTH OF CIVILIZATION
Each 6*s*. *net*.
THE CHILDREN OF THE SUN
£1 1*s*. *net*.

PETRIE (Sir Flinders)
A HISTORY OF EGYPT
In 6 Volumes.
Vol. I. FROM THE IST TO THE XVITH DYNASTY
Eleventh Edition, Revised.
12*s*. *net*.
Vol. II. THE XVIITH AND XVIIITH DYNASTIES
Seventh Edition, Revised. 9*s*. *net*.
Vol. III. XIXTH TO XXXTH DYNASTIES
Third Edition. 12*s*. *net*.
Vol. IV. EGYPT UNDER THE PTOLEMAIC DYNASTY
By EDWYN BEVAN. 15*s*. *net*.
Vol. V. EGYPT UNDER ROMAN RULE
By J. G. MILNE.
Third Edition, Revised. 12*s*. *net*.
Vol. VI. EGYPT IN THE MIDDLE AGES
By STANLEY LANE POOLE.
Fourth Edition. 10*s*. *net*.

PONSONBY OF SHULBREDE (Lord)
ENGLISH DIARIES £1 1*s*. *net*.
MORE ENGLISH DIARIES
12*s*. 6*d*. *net*.
SCOTTISH AND IRISH DIARIES
10*s*. 6*d*. *net*.

RUTTER (Frank)
EL GRECO. Illustrated. £1 16*s*. *net*.

SELLAR (W. C.) and YEATMAN (R. J.)
1066 AND ALL THAT
Illustrated by JOHN REYNOLDS.
63*rd Thousand*. 5*s*. *net*.

STEVENSON (R. L.)
THE LETTERS Edited by Sir SIDNEY COLVIN. 4 Vols. *Each* 6s. *net.*

STOW (G. W.) and BLEEK (Dorothea F.)
ROCK PAINTINGS IN SOUTH AFRICA
Illustrated. £2 2s. *net.*

SURTEES (R. S.)
HANDLEY CROSS
MR. SPONGE'S SPORTING TOUR
ASK MAMMA
MR. FACEY ROMFORD'S HOUNDS
PLAIN OR RINGLETS?
HILLINGDON HALL
Each illustrated. 7s. 6d. *net.*
JORROCKS'S JAUNTS AND JOLLITIES
HAWBUCK GRANGE
Each illustrated. 6s. *net.*

TAYLOR (A. E.)
PLATO: THE MAN AND HIS WORK
£1 1s. *net.*
PLATO: TIMÆUS AND CRITIAS
6s. *net.*
ELEMENTS OF METAPHYSICS
12s. 6d. *net.*

TILDEN (William T.)
THE ART OF LAWN TENNIS
Revised Edition.
SINGLES AND DOUBLES
Each illustrated. 6s. *net.*
THE COMMON SENSE OF LAWN TENNIS
MATCH PLAY AND THE SPIN OF THE BALL
Each illustrated. 5s. *net.*

TILESTON (Mary W.)
DAILY STRENGTH FOR DAILY NEEDS
Thirty-fourth Edition. 3s. 6d. *net.*
India Paper. *Leather,* 6s. *net.*

TRAPP (Oswald Graf)
THE ARMOURY OF THE CASTLE OF CHURBURG
Translated by J. G. MANN.
Richly illustrated.
Limited to 400 copies.
£4 14s. 6d. *net.*

UNDERHILL (Evelyn)
MYSTICISM. *Revised Edition.* 15s. *net.*
THE LIFE OF THE SPIRIT AND THE LIFE OF TO-DAY 7s. 6d. *net.*
MAN AND THE SUPERNATURAL
7s. 6d. *net.*
THE GOLDEN SEQUENCE 7s. 6d. *net.*
CONCERNING THE INNER LIFE
2s. *net.*
THE HOUSE OF THE SOUL 2s. *net.*

VARDON (Harry)
HOW TO PLAY GOLF
Illustrated. *Nineteenth Edition.*
5s. *net.*

WELD-BLUNDELL (Dom B.)
SELF-DISCIPLINE AND HOLINESS
5s. *net.*

WILDE (Oscar)
THE WORKS
In 16 Vols. *Each* 6s. 6d. *net.*
I. LORD ARTHUR SAVILE'S CRIME AND THE PORTRAIT OF MR. W. H.
II. THE DUCHESS OF PADUA
III. POEMS
IV. LADY WINDERMERE'S FAN
V. A WOMAN OF NO IMPORTANCE
VI. AN IDEAL HUSBAND
VII. THE IMPORTANCE OF BEING EARNEST
VIII. A HOUSE OF POMEGRANATES
IX. INTENTIONS
X. DE PROFUNDIS AND PRISON LETTERS
XI. ESSAYS
XII. SALOME, A FLORENTINE TRAGEDY, and LA SAINTE COURTISANE
XIV. SELECTED PROSE OF OSCAR WILDE
XV. ART AND DECORATION
XVI. FOR LOVE OF THE KING
5s. *net.*
XVII. VERA, OR THE NIHILISTS

WILLIAMSON (G. C.)
THE BOOK OF FAMILLE ROSE
Richly Illustrated. £8 8s. *net.*